# BETWEEN TWO RIVERS

## Selected Poems 1956-1984

## MAURICE KENNY

## WHITE PINE PRESS

*ABV-589/*

*PS*
*356/*
*F49*
*B47*
*/987*

# ACKNOWLEDGEMENTS

*9/1988*
*amsh*

The author wishes to express gratitude to the editors and publishers of the presses which first published the books in this volume:

*The Hopeless Kill* Privately printed, 1956

*Dead Letters Sent* Troubador Press, 1958

*I Am the Sun* Akwesasne Notes, 1973; dodeca, 1976; White Pine Press, 1979

*North: Poems of Home* Blue Cloud Quarterly Press, 1979; White Pine Press, 1981

*Only as Far as Brooklyn* Good Gay Poets, 1981

*Kneading the Blood* Strawberry Press, 1981

*Boston Tea Party* Soup Press, 1982

*The Smell of Slaughter* Blue Cloud Quarterly Press, 1982

*Blackrobe: Isaac Jogues* North Country Community College Press, 1982

*The Mama Poems* White Pine Press, 1984


Front cover drawing by Rokwaho.

Title page drawing by Wendy Rose.

ISBN 0-934834-73-3

Published by White Pine Press
76 Center Street
Fredonia, New York 14063

# BETWEEN TWO RIVERS

Maurice Kenny

# BETWEEN TWO RIVERS
## SELECTED POEMS 1956-1984

### *THE MAMA POEMS* (1984)

*In memory of my mother, Doris; my father, Andrew;*
*for my sisters Agnes and Mary,*
*and for my granddaughter, Kaherawaks*

. . .

*and in the spirit of "Aunt" Flo Graves,*
*without whom I would not be a poet . . .*

.
. . .

*also for Bro. Benet, Dennis and Elaine, Steve, and Madge and Murry;*
*a special thanks to Rokwaho for his creativity;*
*in loving memory of Mary, Fred and Quino*
*and for the many who rode beside me on the bus . . .*

# *PRELUDE*

To my creative spirit, it indeed seemed odd that a new book of my poems was about to enter the jaws of a press, and I did not have any new words in it. This predicated the mulling of a 'prelude' to express an abiding and deeply-felt appreciation to those who have aided and abetted my years and successes as a writer.

My first poems were composed between two rivers—the St. Lawrence and the Black—somewhere between the ages of eight and fourteen. They were the songs of a shy, young boy, and I sang them to winds and clouds, the horse I rode, the creeks I fished, or the willow I sat beneath. Later, I learned to write them down and sent a few off to newspapers in the area. I went off to New York City and lived in the shadows of writers whose work I then admired, especially those who had survived in Greenwich Village: Edna St. Vincent Millay, e.e. cummings, Eugene O'Neill, and Edmund Wilson, who had a home in upstate New York not far from mine and who sent me a postcard in response to my query stating he "did not see young writers." No longer a boy, but still young, I traveled by sheer accident into the mid-west where I forgot my early pleasures in the poems of Robert Frost almost immediately and delighted in the poetry of William Carlos Williams, Louise Bogan, Dylan Thomas, Edwin Arlington Robinson, A. E. Houseman, Gerard Manley Hopkins, and Denise Levertov—all of whom were galaxies away from my world.

I became acquainted with Blake, Wordsworth, and Keats. Wordsworth held a firm grip on me for years: I've always contended that my worst poetry was that influenced by him. Entering Butler University as a special student, I was soon indoctrinated by the Keats scholar Werner Beyer—who found me a rough thorn—and by Roy Marz, the religious poet. Roy felt I should turn my craft to prose fiction and away from poetry, and I privately turned, in letters, to John Crowe Ransom. He confirmed Marz' contention and added that I had no "sense of rhythm," meaning, naturally, his rhythms. I worked to complete a novel and was immediately discontented with it. I left Butler with Werner Beyer's blessing, and though without a cap and gown, I felt I led Pegasus by the reins. To this moment I feed on his advice.

Shortly after, I entered St. Lawrence University, where I took a course with the fine novelist Douglas Angus. He almost instantly pursuaded me back to poetry, and I will always be thankful to him. I returned to New York City to enter Columbia University on the strength of my father's urging. I passed a rigorous entrance examination in April of 1957 and took a job with the Marboro Book Store chain as a clerk. I was made a shop manager a month or two after employment, and that postponed my entering Columbia. In fact, I never did enter Columbia.

In autumn, 1958, I entered New York University to study with Louise Bogan. There was a sparkle in the air at that time, and a few of those sparks ignited me. Poetry was being born: Allen Ginsberg had published "Howl"; LeRoi Jones (Amiri Baraka) was writing poems and publishing his magazine *Yugen*. All sorts of little magazines were being printed, such as Tuli Kupferberg's *YEAH!*, in which I published a poem. Bob Wilson opened his Phoenix Book Shop, which was soon to be the first bookstore to place my work for sale. Sam Loveman also operated a second-hand book store in the Village. Oscar Williams walked up and down 8th Street with copies of his published anthologies in his armpits. Ezra Pound was released from St. Elizabeth's and one afternoon wandered into the Marboro Shop, stood before the poetry shelf, smiled to see his books in place, and briskly left. Muriel Rukeyser was attaining her peak and was a frequent visitor to the store, as was Paddy Chayefsky, who later became a friend. There was more than a sparkle in the heavens; there was a fire.

Poetry readings were being held all over this magical city, especially in Village coffeehouses and numerous churches. I applied to the Cafe Bizarre and Cafe Borgia to read my poems and was refused because the coordinators said I didn't look like a poet. (In those days I was forced to wear a white shirt and tie because of my job.) I was then living in a loft on Bleeker and Lafayette Streets, and in the building I had a young, French friend, Yves Bolomet, who was a rather sensual, handsome youth and looked the way a poet was expected to look. I wrote anti-flag poems and Yves read them at the readings; we split the passed-hat. There was fire, and sparkle and combustion.

No longer a boy—in fact, by then I was certainly losing that blush of youth altogether—I remained, however, shy and somewhat terrified of the literary scene. I remember meeting Jack Micheline (we shared a publisher) and being intimidated by his firm assurance, and I was totally awed by Asa Renveniste, who was not only a published poet, but published in Europe. I met Sam Loveman at this time, again at the Marboro shop, who took me under his wing, and, by coincidence, Willard Motley, the then- famous novelist. I was corresponding with Marianne Moore in Brooklyn and William Carlos Williams in New Jersey. I had become acquainted with the great, but I remained a shadowy figure looking in—a hungry man staring through the window at the diners.

Through Sam's auspices, I met Venable Herdon, who was co-editing *Chelsea Magazine*. I was tongue-tied. Herdon fervently wished to publish some "fragments" of Hart Crane's work never before published. They were in Sam's safekeeping, and he offered them to the magazine on the proviso that *Chelsea* also print my poems. Poor, good Sam. He lost. I don't know if Venable ever did acquire Crane's "fragments."

I did manage to place a few pieces in sporadic journals; I wrote drama reviews for Ed Corley's *Off-Broadway Magazine*, and taught a course in the history of drama at Mary Tarcai's School of Drama. Mary introduced me to many theatre people, but again the country bumpkin was totally tongue-cuffed and missed some terrific opportunities. Mary could not come to terms with my reluctance to hustle her theatrical friends— who were perfectly willing to be hustled. I'm sure with the hay still clinging to my hair and my north country accent, I was a respite from the fraudalent poses of their sophisticated salons.

I was comfortable with Paddy—I allowed him to do all the shouting—and with Sam Loveman, who wasn't as shy as I was but was certainly discreet. I spent many evenings with Sam in either his large apartment over the famous fish shop on upper Second Avenue or in the East 86th Cafeteria. With Sam I held my own; he actually listened to what I had to say and approved of my poetry. He believed I was another Hart Crane. I was not. Nor did I wish to be. It was a thrill to know this kind, informative man and to have him write the introduction for my first book, *Dead Letters Sent*.

But to fill in the gaps and set the tenor of my times, I have been rambling through a past and neglecting what I had set out to remember: Louise Bogan. Nearly thirty years later, it seems that her class on that first night was outrageously large— somewhere near fifty students, and we had been screened! I remember a few stood against the wall. Looking back, it seems to me that Louise was always dressed in black with lace at the collar. This reflection may simply be due to the fact that I remember her as being a very sad, pained woman, and I mistakenly shroud her in black cloth. She entered the classroom quietly with a few books clutched to her breast and holding a handkerchief to her mouth. She was never without that handkerchief—at least in class. She coughed into it a good deal of the time. I recognized instantly that she was my kind of woman: she was not merely shy, but was actually intimidated by her students. She did not enjoy teaching, and I soon gathered that she taught because of finances, even though she was in demand on the speaking circuit and often missed class to give a reading or a speech. Her substitute was always Donald Allen, who was then editing his classic anthology, *New American Poetry*.

The first evening, Louise announced that she could not teach us poetry, that no one could, it was not teachable, and that about all she could offer was how to punctuate and capitalize. She proceeded to do exactly that for he entire semester. We read our poems in class and the students made critical comments. She took them home, presumably read them, returned the poems to class, and occasionally made pronouncements—if that is not too harsh a word—on poems which exemplified particular ideas. She spoke of numerous contemporary poets; Allen Ginsberg's "Howl," she had decided, would get, if fortunate, a footnote in the literary history of the time. She often referred to literary politics and how one editor or anthologist could make or break a writer's career and reputation. She was faithful to her beliefs, and her beliefs were strong and deep. Early in the semester I approached her desk after class one night with the book *Poetry and Its Forms* by Mason Long clutched in hand. The handbook aroused her interest, and we marched to the subway together. The next day we met for lunch, and I gave her a copy of the Long book. After that, we met and talked frequently.

It was in these out-of-class sessions that I learned what she had to offer me. It was not so much her praise of my work nor the constructive criticism—and there was a large amount of both—but the suggestions she offered and my careful reading of her own magnificent poems. To her, a tree was not a tree but an elm, a white pine, a birch; a bird was not a bird but a hawk, a titmouse; a river was not a river but the St. Lawrence or the Mohawk. You establish communication by identification. This also aids the reflective juices. The first thought or the first image may be the best, but explore, define and refine, cut away what is not connotative. Fear nothing—not the personal nor the symbolic. Endure with the past, and your own past. Fear nothing knowing the worst shall happen.

Tragic experience was always near Louise Bogan; pain rarely took a holiday. When a youth, I was told that to create a great work of art one needed to suffer, and I always looked for suffering. Louise Bogan never had to look far: it appeared frequently at dawn, the breakfast table, the bedtime pillow. One of her greatest disappointments, a broken dream, was that she was never awarded a Pulitzer, which she adamantly prized and deserved. Louise Bogan was a fine teacher and a masterful poet—truly one of the great 20th century voices.

Upon leaving Louise Bogan's class, I was finished with formal, institutional learning. I was on my own and swimming in white water. Under her influence I had published *Dead Letters Sent* with Brayton Harris at Troubador Press, and shortly after, Aadrvark printed *With Love to Lesbia* and *And Grieve, Lesbia,* both highly imitative of Catullus. I did not publish a collection again until after *Akwesasne Notes*, Alex Jacobs then poetry editor, first printed "I Am The Sun." "Sun" was printed in a pamphlet by dodeca and later again by White Pine Press. In those years I wrote little and published rarely. Much of my time was spent traveling to Mexico, California, the Southwest, Puerto Rico, and the Virgin Islands. I lived for exactly one year in Chicago where I wrote obituaries and advertisements for the Chicago *Sun-Times*. I returned to New York City in 1967, found an apartment in Brooklyn Heights, and took a job as waiter in a posh discoteque on Park Avenue where I was known as Maurice, the French waiter. I worked there on and off until a heart attack stopped work in 1974.

Since 1976 I have published nearly one book a year. Good friends have helped keep me sane and alive, and there are many—some of whom have passed through my time and light and were taken away, some by death and others by chance and interest. I want to thank them all for touching my life and for their teaching. With indulgence, I must give special thanks and large praise to my beautiful niece, Martha Rebeor, and her husband, Rick, for being beautiful, sensitive, and loving. They have sacrificed so much and have drawn our blood ties tighter each summer we picked strawberries in the hot fields, counted the Macintosh apples hanging in the moonlight in their backyard, or made chocolate fudge at the holiday stove. There are other friends/teachers who have remained over good times and sour, and I would enjoy naming names: Wanda and Julian, Wendy and Arthur, Helene and Robert, my two Dianes, Salli and Francis, John and Eva, and least I forget, Dan and Priscilla, Paul, Duane, Louie, Ruth and Larry.

Some of the work in this book has been re-worked, but many of the poems stand as they were first published.


February 1986
Brooklyn Heights

*THE HOPELESS KILL*
*and*
*DEAD LETTERS SENT*
*1956, 1958*

# THE HOPELESS KILL

I went to the forest with my ax
To break the neck of a copperhead.
I found the sleek and lanquid thing
Entangled round a hemlock tree.
His eyes, mere firing flames,
Were peering at a hummingbird
A foot away. I crept across
The autumn haze, could smell the pine
And ferns, and saw a puccoon's white
Shadow illuminate a chip
Of brittle shale.
   I lunged. The ax
Came plunging down. It struck him just
Below the brownish head. He coiled
About the hemlock's trunk; unwound,
And spat his green and evil cud . . .

I laughed. The thing I sought to kill
Was there on embryonic earth,
Was drowning in a pool of blood.
The copperhead was dead. But then
It was too soon to know its mate,
Behind the camouflage of ferns,
Was hatching eggs of many sons.
Nor did I stop to realize
That I must soon return to stalk
The April woods, must live to kill,
To drop the bloody ax again.

## DEAD LETTERS SENT
### (BY THE ONTARIO SHORES)

I

Now the clover greens the long meadow
Running the brook to the sweep of the rising hills;
The corn and wheat, which I have sown
These past few weeks, have shown their first green tongues
Of life; the pear orchard and the leafless patch of vines
Have been pruned and sprayed and there has been
Some time to plant a few hollyhocks
At the gate and some yellow columbine
At the edge of the road. Now there are long
Moments to think of you before the dust
Drives the fields to weeds and the corn leans
In the heat of the sun.

                       I have cursed the sweat,
As you remember well, but still the hoe,
Smoothly worn, has been the friend
No man could ever be. This you
Will understand: for you have known, have gripped
Its power in your hand and fought the muscled earth,
The bugs and even God to get a crop
Grown and into town, have known the hoe
Pressing against the child that did not live
To grow. But then there were the two and empty fields
Or empty womb is not the blinding pain
When two can curse and share the burden of
The contagious hearse that not only
Broke the purse but broke the thing
Between one man and his woman. But this
Does seem unfair: you were more than mere woman.
And now? I wonder how many worms
You are, or if I have split your seed
And left you open to the sun, the calm
Indifference of the quiet moon,
Or the hungry bellies of the stupid birds
That flock and black the fields determined
To see ruin spread and bake the fields and crack
The river beds. You always said to pray
For prayer would overflow the water well
And turn the stone to bread, but I . . . but we
Have broken teeth on stone and prayer puts a thought

In a fellow's head and drives worry from his tongue
To just behind the ear. I have prayed for a thousand rains,
And I prayed for you: the rain seldom came...

II

In the morning I will go to the fields after
The hay has shakened the thick dews, after
The horses are watered and the cows walked to
The high green pasture on the east hills.
With a jug of ginger-beer, some cold beef
And bread, and a bag full of strawberries all swinging
In a bucket on my arm, I will ride
The roan mare to the north lot and see
If I can't mow ten square acres before
The sun has leapt too high and uncontrollable
In the sky.

When I just can't take any more sun,
And sweat, and god-damned flies I'll hunt out your
Cedar by the pile of stones and just ease-off
For and hour and let the sun and bugs
Play all the havoc they think necessary
To finish out their day's chores. When
The berries are gone and the beer is flat and I
Have had myself some little nap and the sun
Leans toward the big red barn then I will lead
The mare back to harness and lead myself
Back to the high seat of the old mower
Where I can play king for an hour, a king
Who can stretch his glance and see as far as he owns,
As far as the stream rolling down 'Witches Hill'
And through the rumpled fields of daisies, clover and rye.
And when my eye is worn-out from staring
And the mare, shaking her mane, is restless to go,
Then I again will mow and I suppose,
Thank God (or whoever it is that spits
The seeds of rain into the earth and pulls
Up the hay and the grain like a robin
Pulling the tail of a worm), will thank this God

11

For the strength of my arm and the power of the mare,
And the rain and wretched heat of the sun, and thank
Whomever God is for the hands that hold
The reins and lower the blade and make sure
It's hay that's cut. Yesterday the blade
Sawed off, neat as you can, the grey head
Of a mouse trying to break an autumn nut
That winter spared. I felt a drop of blood,
Warm and shy, hiss against my cheek.

So all morning long and all afternoon
I'll mow, stopping now and then to give
My horse a rest, and we will work together
Until I see the first bat rise
And streak against the sky.

                       I do not care
To return home and if my horse were not
Tired and if the grazed cows did not
Wait by the locked gate near the barn then I
Would stay within the fields and work all night
By the stars, no matter how dull or how bright.
Home is a house of ghosts and shadows, sounds
Which are restless throughout the long dark night,
Dark even when the moon lies asleep on the pillow.
A man can't take the moonlight in his arms.

## FOUR: IN THE CHINESE MANNER

*1. A Summer Day*

Sun skims across the waves of the quiet bay,
Water swells and pushes
And licks at the shore.
Gulls hunt purple minnows
And fly into the sun
To disappear
With their screams.
Beyond the water-weeds,
Out upon the stepping-stones
Terns shun the day,
And, listening to the rock of water
Slapping hollow-sounding stones,
They breed their young . . .
Their fierce eyes opened to distant sounds
Of dogs barking
In the forest at the running hare.
Dead fish, drying on the hot sand,
Corrode the smell of gentians
And drive ants
To labor in the heat of the moistened hour.
Wind pounds the clouds.
But no one will believe the poet
That the things of summer
Have their evil way.


*2. Tramp: Walking, Walking*

Wind thunders to the fields and the road,
Rain plunders
The once stillness of early night.
I walk alone with the collar of my coat
Turned-up, scratching the lobe of my ear.
My last cigarette burns
Holes in the darkness,
And the weaving trees drip
Chilled water on my nose.
October is meant for the dead,
And only the dead
Can bear
Ambiguous rain.

## 3. At the Bottom Of The Year

Wild mallards shy the mountains,
Holding in the stiff lake
Under the frozen moon,
Perhaps the millionth year;
They do not see
The green leaf red
But feel
Chill
Run the sap.
Leaves are left crisp.

The wise mallard
Has no need
To smell
Or taste the sweet
Apple
To know fruit,
Rusting on the tree,
Waits for one breeze
To push it off the bough.
Mallards' wings know,
And twitch to move south.

Leaves must now
Be told
When to shake
Their green, and blush;
Apples do not know
When to fall
Unless some stick
Reaches through sky
And tips the heavy bough.
Even farmers listen
To the radio
For the first signs of snow.

## 4. Country Scene

Crab apple blossoms
In the orchard.
Wind plays,
Strews the blossoms' scent
About,
Blond children,
At play under the old tree,
Laugh at grass
Ripping the silent earth.
They are pleased
With the song of the thrush
Who sings to his mate
In the nest of straw and mud.

The geese call from woods,
And the barren mare
Neighs at the stone fence
Piled by the side of the road.
The youth takes the hand
Of the girl,
Leads her to the near forest.
Her hair blossoms
With flowers
Of the ancient tree.

And they wait
And listen
For the pain of Spring.

## REALIZATION

You went to play your bingo game
And left me sitting on the railroad track.
I sat, holding a dying rose in my hand,
And cried till I was sick.
Your daughter came from the house
And struck
Me with the stem.
I threw the rose away,
Then dead,
Into a water well by the track
And wiped the blood from my cheek.
I stopped crying,
And knew all roses were dead,
And all daughters
Would strike
My cheek.

# THE HAWK

### For Asa

I rise morning after morning
And walk the wet meadows
Though I never frighten off the hawk
With a gun or with a cry,
But I have sometimes held
It bread and bits of meat
To coax it from the sky.

His talons drip with honey,
His beak is full of gentian leaves
And blossoms, and his eye
Shines with a strange kindness
As his feathers dust the sky.

What drives the babe to suck
And kneads the blood with passion;
What tickles idiots
And has them laugh
Drives my hands to clutch
His feathers and wear
Them in an ancient fashion.

## NOON

Peacocks trampled the strawberries
As rooster crowed, startling the sunning hills;
Sparrows shook the cherries
While the thrush warbled tu whee, tu whee, tu whill.

The rose seduced the unsuspecting moth
And locked him in her petals;
The brook strangled minnows
Just as the calf ripped his hide on nettles.

Margarette fell from her zooming swing,
Peter bumped his button-nose
On the face of the door that wouldn't close
While the hired girl tore her only hose
Climbing a ladder to fetch a ball of string.

...

At noon wine was dust in bottles,
And cream soured in the jars;
At noon sun was red with blisters
And Crazy-Lou could not find the stars.

What a world with peacocks in berries;
Broken children in despair;
What a world without midnight fairies
To blow magic across Spring air.

*I AM THE SUN*
*1976*

# I AM THE SUN

A Song of Praise, Defiance and Determination

*"I did not know then how much was ended. When I look back from this high hill of old age, I can see the butchered women and children lying heaped and scattered along the crooked gulch as plain as when I saw them with eyes still young. And I can see that something else died there and was buried in the blizzard. A people's dream died there. It was a beautiful dream . . . the nation's hoop is broken and scattered."*

—Black Elk

Father, I come;
Mother, I come;
Brother, I come;
Father, give us the arrows.

*Chankpe Opi Wakpala!.*

Father, I hold one for Big Foot;
Mother, I hold one for Black Coyote;
Brother, I hold one for Yellow Bird;
Father, give us back the arrows.

*Chankpe Opi Wakpala!*

Father, give us sky;
Father, give us sun in the east;
Father, give us night in the west;
Father, watch our shadows;
Father, give us back our arrows.

*Chankpe Opi Wakpala!*

Mother, your breast is bare;
Mother, your breast was not enough to sustain us;
Mother, hold our bones now;
Mother, we search for our arrows.

*Chankpe Opi Wakpala!*

Brother, we cried for you;
Brother, we called you back;
Brother, we descended with you,
    and your flesh
    and your bones
    and your fur which kept us warm;
Brother, when our arrows are returned
    we will seek you.

*Chankpe Opi Wakpala!*

Arrows, now the skies are diseased;
Arrows, now the earth is diseased;
Arrows, now the people are sick on dreams;
Arrows, come back to us.

*Chankpe Opi Wakpala!*

Our father is gone;
Our father has fled;
Our father has turned his face;
Arrows give us back our father.

Our mother has closed her eyes;
Our mother has closed her mouth;
Our mother has closed her heart;
Arrows, give us back our mother.

Our brother has wandered away;
Our brother does not walk;
Our brother has gone down;
Arrows, give us back our brother.

The arrows broke at Greasy Grass;
The arrows broke with Crazy Horse;
The arrows broke with Sitting Bull;
Father, give us back our arrows.

*Chanke Opi Wakpala!*

In the river of his blood,
    I stand in Bigfoot's grave;
In the shout of fear,
    I shout for Black Coyote;
In the dance of his dream,
    I dance for Yellow Bird;
Father, give us back our arrows.

We will put the center back
    in your country;
We will circle stones and make the hoop
    in your country;
We will plant the seed of the sacred tree
    in your country.

We will fill the river with water;
We will fill the woods with trees;
We will clothe the bones with flesh;
We will empty the graves;
We will call back the the wolf, the deer;
We will build the walls of the dream;
We will make and tend the fire,
    in your country.

For I am the sun!

I am the sun!

I stand above the world.

*Chankpe Opi Wakpala!*
*Chankpe Opi Wakpala!*

Father, give us back our arrows,
        and make a woman into a child,
                a boy into a man,
                a girl into a woman,
                an arrow into a country,
                a country into a home.
                a home into the sun.

*Chankpe Opi Wakpala!*
*Chankpe Opi Wakpala!*
*Chankpe Opi Wakpala!*

Father, give us no more graves;
Father, give us back our arrows!
We have learned to hold them sacred!


*Note: This chant is based upon a Lakota-Sioux Ghost Dance song. *Chankpe Opi Wakpala* is Lakota-Sioux meaning Wounded Knee.

*NORTH: POEMS OF HOME*
*1977*

## FIRST RULE

stones must form a circle first not a wall
open so that it may expand
to take in new grass and hills
tall pines and a river
expand as sun on weeds, an elm, robins;
the prime importance is to circle stones
where footsteps are erased by winds
assured old men and wolves sleep
where children play games
catch snowflakes if they wish;
words cannot be spoken first

as summer turns spring
caterpillars into butterflies
new stones will be found for the circle;
it will ripple out a pool
grown from the touch
of a water spider's wing
words cannot be spoken first

that is the way to start
with stones forming a wide circle
marsh marigolds in bloom
hawks hunting mice
boys climbing hills
to sit under the sun to dream
of eagle wings and antelope;
words cannot be spoken first

## COLD CREEK

trout speckled in April dawn
slivered with silver of early spring . . .
song poured to the willows of daylight
over the sandy banks of the creek
cold to the toe, cold to the boy
caught like rainbow trout
by the hook in the jaw;
song poured to the grass, minnows
burnished in the leaping of noon
over and down the hills, quarried
and crushed in the fist of the pimple
that would claim me to manhood,
manhood shied like rats
in the haybarn seeking blood
not the hen's eggs mama said;
song poured to the flowing creek,
jumping rocks, staggering down dams,
thrusting weight against stones;
song poured to the winds
that bristled my cowlicks and burnt
goosepimples into the flesh of my thighs;
song poured into the night willows
with only shadows under

then words crept out like mice in the dark,
and Cold Creek, that had leaped from a hill
a spring, turned and entered the wide river
with my song

# SWEETGRASS

### For Jerome & Diane Rothenberg

Seeded in the mud on turtle's back
Greened in the breath of the west wind
Fingered by the children of the dawn
Arrowed to the morning sun
Blessed by the hawk and sparrow
Plucked by the many hands in the laughter
   of young girls and the art of old women

You hold the moments of the frost and the thaw
You hold the light of the star and the moon
You hold the darkness of the moist night
   and the music of the river and the drum
You are the antler of the deer
You are the watery fire of the trout
You are the dance of the morning
You are the grunts and the groans
   the whimpers and whistles of the forest

You are the blood of the feet
   and the balm for the wound
You are the flint and the spark
You are the child of the loins
   and the twin of the armpit
You are the rock of the field
   and the great pine of the mountain
You are the river that passes in the burnt afternoon
You are the light on the beak and the stump
   and the one-legged heron in the marsh
You are the elk in the snow
You are the groundhog and the bear
You are the claw of the muskrat

You are the ache in the spine
   yet the scent of summer
You are the plum and the squash and the gooseberry
   the flower of the bean
You are the bark of the house

You are the rainbow
   and the parched corn in your woven basket
You are the seed of my flesh
   and I am the flesh of your seed

## HEAVY WINTER
*For Peter Blue Cloud*

stone spruce
glisten on moon meadows
of north country

winter steel
glaze trunk and branch
reflect the axe

stars mingle
within needles
points touch the snout
of the coy-dog on the hill

the nearby farmhouse
is dark and empty
the barn collapsed
the horse cold


## BLACK RIVER

drowned in the pool of bullheads
caught in the power of blades
of paper mills and pleasure boats

mama wouldn't scale the fish
for the summer pan and the pain
in his stomach and the ache in his eye
when she threw them back in the river
black in the hard thoughts of men
black in the terror in its pools
that whirled the life of kids eager
for fish and the hardy slap of pop's hand
on the proud shoulder for having victored
the mighty prowess of the river, black
black in the night when only an arm surfaced
and his toys were given away, and clothes burnt

black river, Black River, I hear the groans
of your throat . . . these many years

# IN NORTH COUNTRY GRAVEYARDS

My fingers in the earth . . . I could hear
   they spoke but not to men
   nor serpents sleeping in the grass . . .
   they spoke to blood and fingertips
   to wind and deer leaping on the wind

My fingers in the earth . . . I could hear
   like spider who led them from the dark
   I took the withered hands
   and approached this cross of roads:
   a hawk sat under the circle of the sun
   a straight arrow in its beak;
   a field mouse lay by the hawk's talons
   nibbling a fresh berry
   green corn grew from its grey ear

My fingers in the earth . . . I could see
   a wolf in the clearing of the woods
   a bloody bone clenched between its jaws
   a nest of pheasant feathers at its feet . . .
   a wolf who had not roamed these hills
   for a hundred years or more
   had gone north into Canada with moose and bear
   long before my mouth had touched my mother's breast
   long before my grandmother wrapped her bones in grass

My fingers in the earth . . . I could hear
 they spoke but not to men
 nor serpents sliding in the grass
 they spoke to blood and fingertips
 to trillium, sparrow fledglings in the elms
My fingers in the earth . . . I could see
                   I could hear!

## OWL'S HEAD
*Near Malone, N.Y.*

### For Raribokwats

New moon on winter grass
snow on the northern moon;
the lead light of the kerosene lamp
drops through the window onto snow,
coy-dogs howl

the grey cat from Hogansberg
creeps through the dusty dark
seeking soft flesh of mice
nibbling postage stamps
in the lower draw of the desk

Reddog pisses on the snow . . .
maybe he remembers
long ago Sitting Bull was murdered today;
in heavy boots, Dorothy
stirs soup, bakes biscuits;
Snowbird adds up the pains of the day

chored, Dorothy takes time out to laugh;
in her fear of mice, Snowbird brushes
away the night, the cat and goes to bed;
Reddog smokes and talks of Christians

I suggest they tie a rope
from the house-door to the pine
for in a blizzard they'd never
get back to the woodstove;
Dorothy smiles

mutely we say goodnight
climb the dark to ourselves;
the mountains say nothing.

# HOME
### For Rick

North
        north by the star
hills under, cows, brush
river broken by spring
men broken by harvest and stone
fields and fields of stone
stone tall as a boy
boys tall as crab apple
spruce weighted with moonshine

north
        north by the star
starlight that parts the corn
starlight that glimmers on autumn
squash and beans
apples caught by the frost
frosty women hanging clothes
balloon in the tight sharp air
pine-stove melts those figures, fingers

north
        north by the star
old men smoke in a circle
north by the village
men smoke in a circle
over the feathers of a partridge
that drummed on the floor of the forest
deviled in the ambush of the wind

north
        north by the star
we go home, we go . . .
to the pheasant, woodchuck, muskrat
the last deer standing the summer
of flies on the blood of the wolf
howled in the north
                    north by the star
starring the Adirondacks
forgotten in the rush for campsites
brown bear mussled to honey-
cookies tourist tease
to the crackling of their arms

and the butchery of the bear
who will not share the berry picking
with the girls of June this year
in the north, north
                    by the north star
hills under, brush, cabins, towns
rivers broken by spring

we go home to the north
                    north by the star

## NORTH
### In Memory of My Father

sun rises over mountain lakes
fox breakfasts in the berry patch
mice tug grains into the burrow
grass has a way of growing

north by the old trail
north by the Susquehanna
north by the Freeway
north by the Alleghany or Mohawk
airlines that sweep you into north country,
deerland, Thousand Islands;
north by semis that scoop up the north
and wrap its aluminum soil about
your Thanksgiving turkey
and freeze your pudding in the refrigerator

north by any path would be north
north . . . by north star, northern
northern country of villages and cowpens
cheese factories and crab apples, trout
diseased elms and sick roots
fenced meadows slit by snowmobiles
sky cracked by television wires,
and hunters blizzard to cabins
by dead deer . . . the last kept
them abandoned in the north snow
from home in Staten Island

north of strawberry fields, milkweed
north of maples running sap to boil
north, north country, northern New York
where corn grew to the table and squash
and bean covered the valleys
north of strawberry fields, north of sumac
north of smoke, north of tomorrow, today
of yesterday that was and is and will be
for strawberries grow forever
and wolves will cross the frozen river
under the flight of geese

sun humps over hills and horses
muskrats in the stream
swimming to shore with a mouthful of mud
the bee sipping honey
minnows in the creek

grass has a way of growing
north, north along the old trail

guard the eastern gate

# LAND
## 1976

Torn, tattered, yet rugged
in the quick incline of bouldered hills
crab appled, cragged, lightning-struck birch, cedar;
wilderness muzzled; forests . . . kitchen tables and bedposts
of foreign centuries; meadows cowed
beyond redemption, endurance, violated
by emigres' feet, and vineyards alien
to indigenous squash and berry,
fragile lupine and iris of the pond;
while wounded willows bend in the snow
blown north by the west wind


## 1820

spring lifts under drifts, saplings
hold to the breeze, larks sing, strawberries
crawl from under snow, woodchucks run
stone walls of new cemeteries and orchards;
apples blossom, thistle bloom

(Madame de Feriet's ghost prowls the miraged bridge
spanning Black River and her mansion lanterns
glow in the clear darkness of the French dream,
hazeled in the richness of her opulence

the lands she would hold out to tenants for rent
have neither clearings nor plows;
the disillusionment loried her trunks to France,
her mansion to ashes, her bridge to dust in 1871,
her savings to pittance, her dream to agony

Madame de Feriet gave her French aristocratic manner
to a signpost at the edge of the county road,
tangled now by yellow roses and purple vetch)

*1976*

April lifts from under the drifts of grey
snow piled by plows ruthless in their industrial
might to free roads and make passage
for trucks and automobiles to hurry to the grave
with dead horses in the far pasture
that no longer sustains the hunger of bleating lambs

virgin spring lifts, its muddy face scarred
and mapped with trails of progress, its smoke
rising in pine, maple, flowering aspen,
chicory weed and clods, manure of waste, whey,
abandoned farm houses and barns shaking in the wind . . .
blind old men caught without canes in the storm;
spring bloody in its virginity, its flow corrupted,
raped in zoned courts of law that struck quarried hills . . .
a great god's lance thrust in the quickness of electric sun

rage of spring rivers, swollen with anger . . .
cold voice growling through the night . . . swirling,
swallowing the soft shoulders of shoreline;
the rage of the aged shackled to history
and the crumbling bones of its frame, fisted against
the night, shaking the cane against the dark, the bats
fluttering in the balmy summer eve, fireflies creeping
through the young green grass of the long fresh meadows

*1812*

the north, the north aches in the bones, the land,
in the elms' limbs gently singing in that August
breeze, bereft of holiday and festival, ghost and voice . . .
tunneled by gophers; ticks and fleas stuck to an old dog's back

(General Brown marched his men to Sacketts Harbor,
struck the British in the red belly
and went home to lift a pint to his deeds
and captured acres, to ville a town, erect a fence)

*1976*

the gooseberry is diseased, and the elm,
stone walls broken, sky cracked, pheasants
and young muskrats sterilized, and fields

# MULLEINS ARE MY ARMS

mulleins are my arms
and chicory
the sinew of my flesh;
May strawberries
are the blood of my legs
and the sun of summer;
maples are my head
and the sugar the sap of my tongue
that runs in the warm wind;
crocus are my eyes;
turtle the feet of my winter

seasons are a rumble of
herded old cows
coming to barn from pastures
before snow covers corn,
and the mare jumps the fence
crazy from glittering stones

marvelous is the miracle of spring
and, also, the weight of winter;
the plum which ripens,
drops seeds into pockets of earth
vacated by gophers;
the rabbits that sleep,
and the bear

incredible is the force of April,
and the lust of January;
in the summer of the second year
mulleins grow another branch,

chicory spreads to another field

# DANCING BACK STRONG
# THE NATION
# *1979, 1981*

*". . . Looking back . . . I will know."*
—Karoniaktatie

*Listen . . .*
*The old woman*
            *came here*
      *she brought seeds*
            *in her finger nails*
      *she brought wind*
      *she brought children*
*The old woman*
            *came here*
      *we came here*

## GOING HOME

The book lay unread in my lap
snow gathered at the window
from Brooklyn it was a long ride
the Greyhound followed the plow
from Syracuse to Watertown
to country cheese and maples
tired rivers and closed paper mills
home to gossipy aunts . . .
their dandelions and pregnant cats . . .
home to cedars and fields of boulders
cold graves under willow and pine
home from Brooklyn to the reservation
that was not home
to songs I could not sing
to dances I could not dance
from Brooklyn bars and ghetto rats
to steaming horses stomping frozen earth
barns and privies lost in blizzards
home to a Nation, Mohawk
to faces I did not know
and hands which did not recognize me
to names and doors
my father shut

## IN THE FLOW

*For Bro. Benet*

I learn water
  in the sky
clouds surface
  over sycamores
minnows nibble
  a drowned butterfly

I learn rivers
  by sitting still
watch the crevice
  of my brow
hear wind ripple
  break reflections

I learn water
  in the summer
fox trek down to drink
  autumn whispers

Eye catches
  the hawk
in the winter
  sky

## LEGACY

my face is grass
                    color of April rain;
arms, legs are the limbs
                    of birch, cedar;
my thoughts are winds
                    which blow;
pictures in my mind
                    are the climb uphill
                    to dream in the sun;
                    hawk feathers, and quills
                    of porcupine running
                    the edge of the stream
                    which reflects stories
                    of my many mornings
                    and the dark faces of night
                    mingled with victories
                    of dawn and tomorrow;
corn of the fields and squash . . .
                    the daughters of my mother
                    who collect honey
                    and all the fruits;
meadow and sky are the end of my day
                    the stretch of my night
                    yet the birth of my dust;
my wind is the breath of a fawn
                    the cry of the cub
                    the trot of the wolf
                    whose print covers
                    the tracks of my feet;
my word, my word,
                    loaned
legacy, the obligation I hand
                    to the blood of my flesh
                    the sinew of the loins
to hold to the sun
                    and the moon
which direct the river
                    that carries my song
                    and the beat of the drum
to the fires of the village
                    which endures.

# *FAYE*

wind calls a flute in the pine
wind drums in the needles

a girl waits for a boy
who will come

the girl waits
for the boy

with a mug of sweet tea
and a far gaze;

snow fills the woods
as the girl waits

for the boy
while the pine fire

in the pot-belly stove
warms a dog too old for rabbits

# DRUMS

*listen . . .*

*drums drum*
            *dance dance*
*rattles rattle*
            *sing sing*
*drums dance*
*rattles sing*
*pause and*
            *dance and*

*drums drum*
*to the song*
            *of the young*
                        *warriors*

*listen . . .*

*thunder thunders*
                        *shakes*
*thunder shakes the floor*

# DANCE

*listen . . .*
*a hundred feet*
*a hundred feet*
            *move move*
            *move move*
*from the ancients*
*into Grandfather's shoes*
            *move move*
            *a hundred feet*
            *move move*


*We come*
*We come to greet*
*We come to greet and thank*
    *the strawberry plants*
                        *growing*
                        *growing there*
                        *as tall*
                        *as tall as high*
                        *as tall as high grasses*
                                        *grasses*
        *mice in the grass*
        *chicory in the fields*
        *owl on a branch*

*We come*
*We come to greet and thank*
*We come*
        *to dance*

# THE STEEL WORKER
### For Peter

In the hot Brooklyn night we stood
at a bar drinking beer, and he said,

> "Riding the sky on steel girders
> solid under my feet, wind balances;
> beer tastes good after work
> in these neighborhood bars on Nevins St.,
> but with all the big wages
> there is nothing to pray to
> here in the Brooklyn ghetto
> where my kids don't know
> if they're Black or Puerto Rican;
> too many bars on Nevins St., too many beers
> make me dizzy; I forget to sing
> and will slip one noon
> from those high steel girders."

And he took hold the shadowed hands
of Wolf and Bear and Turtle.


# MOCCASIN

*Listen . . .*

*moccasin moccasin*
            *circle circle*
            *dance dance*
*drums drum*
            *pound pound*
*rattles rattle*
            *sing sing*

*wind howls like a wolf on the hill*

*thunder thunders*
            *shake shake*

*wind sings in the cold air*

*moccasin moccasin*
           *move move*

*wind howls*
*wind sings*
           *leaves fall in the frost*
           *apples ripen in the frost*
           *wolves seek lairs in the frost*
           *snow falls*
           *hills rise*
           *sun sets*
                *sun sun*
                     *sets*

*moccasin moccasin*
           *circle circle*
           *dance dance*

*We come to greet and thank*
                *the winds*
                *the birds*
                *the snow*
                *the drum*
                *the drummer*
                *the dance*
                *the dancer*
           *move move*
           *sun move*
           *moccasin*

## YAIKNI
*Strawberry Moon*

a fierce serpent's tail
lies across my legs;
its mouth breathes into my mouth
    when elms were sweet
    squash tasted of sun
    corn grew in circles
    outside the village
    near streams where trout
    dove through air for spiders
    and cedar scented afternoon
it has lain upon my back
under the west wind . . .
muskrat in its jaw . . .
more days than needles
on the tamarack
    sweetgrass is for weaving
    and summer berries
    for a child's tongue
    (eagles soared, wolves
    trotted mountain slopes)
a youth will come
and his arrow
will rid my spine of this serpent

. . .

together we will watch
it quiver in the falling dusk
    morning turtle eyes the east
    smoke rises from a house
    though snow covers pine
    the roots are deep
    and will survive winter
the serpent will return to the sea
and though it leaves a fang mark
on my throat it will fade
    bear awakens
    to the smell of crocus;
    it is the time for bathing
    and then for planting
    and for a good smoke by the fire

...
I will talk with the old people
and come May seek the early thistle
and sweet strawberry
and be healed

## IN MY SIXTH AUGUST

My father wades the morning river
tangled in colors of the dawn.
He drags a net through the cold
waters; he spits tobacco juice,
stumbles. Light warns the minnows
that hide under bullheads. Sharp air
smells of wild lobelia and apple.

In my sixth August a kingfisher
rattles from a willow; I am too
busy picking iris in the wet fields
to know a game warden shakes his head
above us on the narrow bridge to home.
The west wind has trapped our scent
and light prisons our mobile hands.

# NORTH IN WINTER
### For Cheri Henson


To go home
    woodchucks preening in the sun
    along Mohawk summer meadows
To go home
    snow piled to Boonville eaves
    Hogansberg beseiged with plows
    and mobile hunters
To go home
    is always hard
    when the tongue is not always on the handshake
    when the dance is not on the feet
    when the drum has been silent
    and old uncles do not offer your thirst a beer
To go home
    where no hands braid the hair
    nor ask for a song in the Longhouse
    where your grandmother's bones
    are not buried under wind in the grass

Home is where cousins marry
    and sons take deer or rabbit to supper
To go home
    there are mountains and pine
    thistle down, memories of things finished.

A dying bear groans in maple woods.

I went north in winter
                    to dance

        I went north
        when I left
                    it was spring

# WILD STRAWBERRY

### For Helene

And I rode the Greyhound down to Brooklyn
where I sit now eating woody strawberries
grown on the backs of Mexican farmers
imported from the fields of their hands,
juices without color or sweetness

> my wild blood berries of spring meadows
> sucked by June bees and protected by hawks
> have stained my face and honeyed
> my tongue . . . healed the sorrow in my flesh

> vines crawl across the grassy floor
> of the north, scatter to the world
> seeking the light of the sun and innocent
> tap of the rain to feed the roots
> and bud small white flowers that in June
> will burst fruit and announce spring
> when wolf will drop winter fur
> and wrens will break the egg

> my blood, blood berries that brought laughter
> and the ache in the stooped back that vied
> with dandelions for the plucking,
> and the wines nourished our youth and heralded
> iris, corn and summer melon

> we fought bluebirds for the seeds,
> armed against garter snakes, field mice;
> won the battle with the burning sun
> which blinded our eyes and froze our hands
> to the vines and the earth where knees knelt
> and we laughed in the morning dew like worms
> and grubs; we scented age and wisdom

> my mother wrapped the wounds of the world
> with a sassafrass poultice and we ate
> wild berries with their juices running
> down the roots of our mouths and our joy

I sit here in Brooklyn eating Mexican
berries which I did not pick, nor do
I know the hands which did, nor their stories . . .
January snow falls, listen . . .

*ONLY AS FAR AS BROOKLYN*
*1981*

# BOYS
## (Vision)

the hawk flew
to the crazy mountain
plums grew large and red
stained hands and teeth

the crazy mountain shivered
smoke rose from the rocks
the crazy mountain moved,
called hawk, hawk
catch me in your talons

red plums fell to the grass
the hawk told me to go home
they told me I had dreamed
on the crazy mountain
in the time of falling plums

hawk,
I must remember this story
to tell the young boys
fishing in the creek

# I SHALL NOT WRITE OF LOVE

morning's bare shore;
sea plums have no flesh

    I shall marry
    grow cruel with winter,
    dry crisp like chicory
    that hangs above the fire

cats never leave the apartment;
the maid comes on Monday;
the library's usually open

    not that I can't
    but I shall marry

hung over from all that
I bolt the door to intrusions
that peck on windows

    for a while
    if I can resist
    for a while

I shall not write of love.

# WINKTE*

*"He told me that if nature puts a burden on a
man by making him different, it also gives him
a power..."*
—John (Fire) Lame Deer, Sioux Medicine Man

We are special to the Sioux!
They gave us respect for strange powers
Of looking into the sun, the night.
They paid us with horses not derision.

To the Cheyenne we were no curiousity.
We were friends or wives of brave warriors
Who hunted for our cooking pots,
Who protected our tipis from Pawnee.

We went to the mountain for our puberty vision.
No horse or lance or thunderbird
Crossed the dreaming eye which would have sent us
Into war or the hunter's lonely woods.
To some song floated on mountain air,
To others colors and design appeared on clouds,
To a few words fell from the eagle's wind,
And they took to the medicine tent,
And in their holiness made power
For the people of the Cheyenne nation.
There was space for us in the village.

The Crow and Ponca offered deerskin
When the decision to avoid the warpath was made.
And we were accepted into the fur robes
Of a young warrior, and lay by his flesh
And knew his mouth and warm groin;
Or we married (a second wife) to the chief,
And if we fulfilled our duties, he smiled
And gave us his grandchildren to care for.

We were special to the Sioux, Cheyenne, Ponca
And the Crow who valued our worth and did not spit
Names at our lifted skirts nor kicked our nakedness.
We had power with the people!

And if we cared to carry the lance, or dance
Over enemy scalps and take buffalo
Then that, too, was good for the Nation.
And contrary to our stand we walked backwards.


*Sioux word for male homosexual




## APACHE

warrior of the Yamaha
hoteled wild Oakland
in the night of smoke
safe from reservation
eyes and rules . . .
    gentle fingers
    turned back the sheets . . .
warrior of braids
and melon-words
who turned off the whoop
and left apprehension
in the wicki-up
    mouth the color
    of Arizona sunsets;
    body eager,
    more eager than slithering lizards
    on desert rocks . . .
Apache who struck coup on a Mohawk
and left the bed victorious.

EL PASO . . .
*TWO YEARS LATER*
            *For Chuck*

I passed through Billy the Kid
in the desert night;
lights of Lincoln County
bristled like Mexican cigarettes
in the frosty dark

   . . . "stupid". . .

What did you expect to find
a young blond cowboy
standing by the Greyhound depot door
chewing gum, folding the brim
of his white Stetson,
his long smile clenched,
waiting with legs open
for the bus to unload

   . . . "it was stupid". . .

Stupid for Pat Garrett to kill
young Bill with his blond curls
dangling over the winking eye,
his naked toes separated,
his Mexican accent smiling,
fingers scratching his thigh

   . . ."it was stupid, Chuck" . . .
   my saying I'd write . . .

## PAPAGO I

Down into the centuries of your breath
  my centuries prodded

    I meant to leave a song on your ear,
    rabbit fur, a cup of corn,
    a plume, a bowl of apples and warm wind.
    . . .
    I meant to leave my name whispered
    on your mouth because secrets
    are long between your Arizona rocks
    and my old cedar woods of home.
    . . .
    I meant to kindle a campfire
    to warn off wolves which would gnaw
    our bones and carry off our shadows.

Down into the centuries of your blood
  my centuries prodded
unearthed the passions of your veins,
the savage fumblings of my hands
which struck the dawn of your movements
and swept winds through the sunset of my day
breaking sky colors into thin light.

Down into the contours of your flesh
  my flesh prodded
but not without gentleness

    I meant to leave our names scratched into stone
    that no river could erase, nor wind defile.
    . . .
    I meant to leave my arms in your arms
    and take only the gift of your voice
    whispering the motions of my blood,
    the taut muscles of our race.

## YUCHI BRAVE
### For Gene

I felt
your smell
as the room
crowded
with your flesh!

Oklahoma dust . . .
    paint upon your cheek;
Reservation red . . .
    watered by your mother's mad white blood,
    canceled by her curse;
Oklahoma dust . . .
    rubbed into your feet,
    cleaned by your mother's heritage;
Oklahoma dust . . .
    your father kissed that cheek,
    your father loved those feet
    and painted your face bright with earth
    and hung dove feathers from your hair;
Oklahoma dust . . .
    blown by your winds
    strangle, choke in your lungs,
    gaunt arms stretched by priests,
    veined legs drawn across pulpits
    upon which your mother sacrificed
    the beauty of your groin;
Oklahoma dust . . .
    your father paints your liquid vision
    in the alleys of San Francisco
    where you wander with wet voices
    caught in the quick of your ear;
Oklahoma dust . . .
    home is for those who cannot leave.

You entered
the room
with your smile
upon
my mouth!

## GRETA GARBO

The park's darkness
increased
with the cripple's loneness.
The leg, braced, ached.
His coiled fingers
shining
like ice or wax
were as broken
as your heart must be.

Handsomely he smiled, asked the time
and paused to comment on the weather of the night:
he must have known I was a poet,
although he did not pose,
but, fearful, he hid
the brace and mangled hand
as you hide your face
and slouch into the resolution of the dark.
God meant his youth
to be broken,
your beauty aged!
War and time take what they want!
The soldier's memory
of straight leg and fingers
does nothing to erase his pain
and give him the love
he seeks nightly in a Brooklyn Park.
Nor does your glory,
or fame,
or multi-reflections
erase wrinkles or soothe gnarled hands.

## AFTER READING THE GREEK POET

*For Larry*

Cavafy, your young man
with quiet eyes and honey skin
walks along the river
wagging a finger at older men;
then enters the house flushed,
and exits, later, pale and worn
from too many kisses,
as the lover raises the window shade
and his dark eyes watch him as he goes.

## THE COST

*For Fred*

Scanning the ads
April and trillium
wet white extinct
fingering the wants and the want nots
marantas praying the night
green dark thirsty
indexing the needs
the *New York Times*
cannot fulfill . . .
cross out Sunday
turn on the comics, coffee
envelopes pile to the lampshade
daydreams drug dryads and dragons
keep mad wolves in the hills

# UNITED
### For Randy

Moon music moved them together
across nights of bat-darkness,
earth drummed by naked feet
that beats Nevada mountains,
high hills of Mohawk country.

Though old Medicine Men,
prodded by priest and politician,
no longer wear robes;
nor boys, geld and tender,
gather holy corn
nor are celebrated on the warpath
and taken in love by strong warriors . . .
they remain in lodges and languages
where the vision is honored,
and grandfathers know Nations will gather.

Moon music moved them togther;
breechclouts left at the door,
straight firs . . . ponderosa to cedar . . .
naked, spent, broken in deep valleys.
The first frenzied dance finished.
Wovoka shook hands with Cornplanter.
Earth parts for the seed of their firs.

## FLASH FINISH

Mad moments: Beethoven's *Eroica*, Picasso's *Guernica*;
Wars are battled on open plains not tented
Under shirts nor shaded by needles: injections
More poisonous than God's wrath which drove them to earth.

    Montezuma gashed out a quivering heart each day
    And shook feverish in the cold winds of night.

No man can say what a handshake is, nor goodness:
Socrates gladly accepted the cup of poison,
Smiling, talking to the young men and the world
As the sun set; he knew it was time to die.

    The crowd admires the matador who whispers love
    Into the bull's ear as his sword tears its heart.

Platitudes render mouths and hands into clay;
Prove that to hate is more difficult
Than to love for hate takes a lifetime to build,
And love is so often crushed in a single orgasm.

    The dying do not remember the crying faces
    Nor take flowers into the grave.

*KNEADING THE BLOOD*
*1981*

## STRAWBERRYING

morning
broods
       in the wide river
Mama bends
       light
       bleeds
       always
in her days of
       picking
(our fields are stained)

the moon, bats
       tell us'
       to go
in the scent of
       berries

fox
  awaken
          in stars

## CORPSE LEAVING THE HOTEL ST. GEORGE
*Brooklyn, N.Y.*

Hooded eyes
roped feet
life cancelled
caw silenced in the city woods

rolled in black rubber casing
roped tightly so it won't get away
the men carry its dignity
to the van owned and operated
by the city of New York

hooded so it can't see death
(the final cheat)
roped so it won't get away
(as if it wanted to)

the men smile
as they shove
the bundle
into the van marked:
Mortuary Division

we go into those green woods of death
anonymous with a small obit
if we have a cousin on the *Times* staff
our bones
placed probably in the city dump
where rats gnaw testicles

(Hawk, hooded, you wheel, circle
this city now for the first time
it is your city and you belong
to it for the first time)

# HAWK,

crow cries the forest
in laughter shaking great oaks
knocking birch together;
laughs to see me prey
at last as I claw the sun
and kick against the morning moon
half-eaten by dogs
running bloody mouths
through these green woods

I am not a plum, nor woodchuck
and yet I am, I am the bane
of crow who dusts my chin
with black feathers cawing
in the falling light

Hawk,
drop my flesh and bones
I am a berry on the bramble
I am not your prey;
crow has lied in his smile, his joke

He threw sun in your eyes
he makes you howl on the moon

Hawk,
drop me from your talons
or I shall be your scat
left on the dry river mud

## THE PARTS WE KEEP

*In memory of William Mothersell*
*d. August, 1976*

we dropped you into dust
    amongst marigolds

we fed you to April trout
    grass growing in your field

we gave parts to perch, bass
    and moose of north Canada
    the autumn fawn you left
    in alder and hickory woods
    the black rivers of Coleman lanterns
    the winter plow of muscle

we kept you from death
    of bones and sinew
    kept your nails and hair strong
    teeth from falling off the jaw
    gave away beagles, rifles
    rusty muskrat traps

we listen to the wild goose honk;
    you trudge maple, birch
    run the hounds

and we went home to drink
    your laughter in a glass
    or two of whiskey
    an epitaph, an anecdote

there is beauty in death

we insult your nerves
    by grasping them together
    and claiming them tendons of the man
    parts of the human being,
    and in reverse separate
    the joints from the body
    the voice from the tongue

eulogies are usually lies and myths
    fitted together by priests
    trying to pass the dead
    to God, exhorting nature
    decorating flesh and soul

we will not lie
    you were nothing more
    than your colds and fevers
    your fishpoles and guns
    your worn hunting socks and boots
    your grandson's nose
we barely knew the ticking of your clock
    the weather of your dreams
    the smell of your curse
    the taint of your sin
    nor touched the warmth of your blood
    as you welcomed neighbors to supper
    in-laws to bed

we will not legend you into heaven
    nor mock your prayer which raised
    an orange marigold
    and blessed the fawn
    or eel swimming in dark waters . . .
    saying, we come again
                come again
    for a man's history is a record,
    a diary not the wish fulfillments
    of a broken wife, or son
    the hope of the fatherless daughter

there is a miracle in death

we dug the grave
　　brought roses and pompoms
　　mass was said, the high holy mass
　　and the priest dropped absolution
　　on the metal of your coffin
　　six friends nailed it tight
　　and carried your weight into darkness;
　　your steel box denies you to eternity
　　and the commingling of your dust
　　with the marigolds of your garden
　　and the blood
　　of your sire and grandson

we can only kneel at the headstone
　　not hear your curse on the wind
　　nor taste you on the hawk
　　nor catch you on the hook
　　nor scent you on the trillium
　　all your parts have been sealed
　　we have only
　　the roar of your automobile
　　the feel of a handshake

there is a creation in death
　　we have no parts

*BOSTON TEA PARTY*
*1982*

# BOSTON TEA PARTY

*1. Assigned*

*A.*

Night closed as the door exposed candles
in little red jars scattered
about the room smelling of boiling tea,
a special tea of licorice and sassafras.

His hair was festooned with birds,
their songs silenced in the loose strands
weeping down the naked flesh of his back.
Birds hung at his waist
in folds and flow of Polynesian fabric,
purple of the sea, green of the mountain.
Kittens played with twine
balled and fisted on the belly of the floor.

Ship-rolled I moved into the light,
face reddened but altar-calm, took a chair
especially arranged with the only cushion,
and held the mug of enigmatic tea
terrifying in its ambivalence.
What realms would I travel from that brew?
What new worlds discover?
What birds would alight on the hair?
Would snakes peel from the mouth;
would fingers extend into lizard tails;
tongue become an angel of flight?

Tall as a priest or goddess he radiated smiles
over the late hours of the night.
He washed my feet, bathed loins,
presed his mouth to the spirit
he thought he touched in the soul, memory.
He blew feathers on my ribs ,
danced drums on my naked knees, cheekbones;
blessed prayers upon my eyelids.

The night was holy, time late.
Mystery shuddered as he knelt before me
as though asking my hands to bless his life,
confirm my secret powers.

He conjured buffaloes from my feet, armpits.
Rattles banged and shook from my teeth.
An elk reared from the floor,
floated through the glass of the dark window.
Hawks fluttered from my ears to the cracked
ceiling, a chalice trembling as wine
spilled down wretched walls of his heart splitting
in the light of those red votive candles lit
to strike the spirit of my history,
ancestry, my drums and rattles,
my curdling war cry, a bloody scalp raised
in my hands to the triumph of the night,
my face black with victory, the slain spirit
resting a pulsing liver between my teeth.
I was savior and warrior, priest and poet,
fertile and fallow, savage and prophet,
angel of death and apostle of truth.
I was the messenger of gods and demons.
He knew my powers could fathom
the darkness of the light.
I bed in Salem.

His ribs opened for my arrow;
his head split for the tomahawk, the club;
his pain longed for my hands to touch it,
soothe it, mold it into a receptacle, an urn
of blood and ashes stirred with a prayer stick
while my chants chewed the potions
that fettered his brain and soul.

I'd drink his tea and spit out rocks.
I'd suck flesh and spit out frogs.
I would paint kingfishers on his thighs,
deer on his heels, morning-glories on his brow.
I would heat stones and steam off sin.
I would tear fifty pieces of flesh
to feed hummingbirds, and marry his dry bones
with Satan and they would live forever
on my fingertips, an apple bough.

Was I not touching the universe—
a feather in my hair, bells on my ankles.
Was I not master of dark dealings of dryads.
I was to raise the pipe, smoke, allow the puffs
to bathe his priesthood which he would gladly loan to me,
naming me the high priest of his foolish
pagan altar adorned with plastic geraniums and peacock feathers.

Pity the unannointed, the damned.
Absolve the guilty and the hangman.

*B.*

I switched on the bathroom light . . .
it broke the room crawling with roaches.
A canary hung dead in his greasy hair;
his flesh was caked with yellow powder;
his earlobes etched with butterfly wings.
"Turn off the light." His pain pleaded.
The candles were dipped in cats' blood.
My severed spirit had been the sacrifice.
He kissed my ring at the door
with the moon down and the cymbals silent.

*C.*

Boston winds pushed me into dawn,
Dogwood bloomed a street, empty and grey.
The Charles was clean, beautiful
in the morning calm. A boy
rode by on a bicycle, his blond hair
blowing free in the breeze. I was damp
with sweat and dew and could hear
the Transit grumble under my feet.
Aging bones ached, a little arthritic,
I would suppose, probably.
Potassium would help the numbing pain
and a ball to roll in the fist
would keep fingers
limp from rage and the kinks of age
in a world estranged from reality.
I picked a crocus. Its scent was fragile.
An ambulance raced past, a dog gnawed a bone.
I crossed the Charles into the grubby
Boston Commons to stare at the swan boats,
consult the aging statues whitened by pigeon dung.

*2.*

*Radio Interview*

He offered me a glass of holy water
to pacify my hunger, request
for a single cup of black coffee . . .
not allowed in the sanctified confines
where only the smoke of incense curled
from the bowl of Buddha's belly.

Into the microphone he prodded voices
of black witches, magic of an alchemist,
the mystery of a grey guru lean on power
but puffed on adoration.
Gently he questioned my frozen soul.

I revealed only the colors of the day:
forsythia bloomed his April yard,
magnolias striking purple against
the Cambridge sky; the mutability
of the State, its saccharin lies.
I revealed the dirt between my toes,
lice crawling my crotch, wax building
in my ears.
Again I spoke of hunger:
a "Big Mac" would do, instant coffee,
plastic pizza, anything but holy water.

No light hung over my monk's shaped head.
No priest hid behind my coat. He smiled.
At the door he took my hand, pulled my frame
to his, whispered: "I have pain
in my throat. Can you heal the hurt?"
I offered to go home and burn sage.
I had a large can I bought once at the A&P.

Back in Brooklyn listening to the bells
of the Korean Church and the Clark St.
transistors booming out their Sunday Mass
to pigeons and shopping-bag women,
I turned on TV and watched the Marx Brothers
cavort in the old farce, "Horse Feathers."

May 6, 1980

*THE SMELL OF SLAUGHTER*
*1982*

# SACRIFICE

*For Joe & Carol*

wolf tracks
on the snow

I follow between
tamarack and birch

cross the frozen creek
dried mulleins
with broken arms
stand in shadows

tracks move uphill
deeper into snowed conifers

I hurry to catch up
with his hunger

cedar sing in the night
of the Adirondacks
he huddles under bent
red willow
panting

I strip in the cold
wait for him to approach
he has returned
to the mountains

partridge drum
in the moonlight
under black spruce

## BOYHOOD COUNTRY CREEK

curved,
changed
by wind
mostly
with hands
and light machinery

rabbits,
muskrats
abandoned cattails
and the smell
of slaughter

mallards,
rainbow trout
speckle
only the memory

bank,
red willow
gave the sandy earth
to a parking lot

voices,
daydreams
merge
into reflection

the air of water
the breath of soil
the sheen of iris
blotted,
the blood
of the hunted

# CORN PLANTER

I plant corn four years:
ravens steal it;
rain drowns it;
August burns it;
locusts ravage leaves.

I stand in a circle and throw seed.
Old men laugh because they know the wind
will carry the seed to my neighbor.

I stand in a circle on planted seed.
Moles burrow through the earth
and harvest my crop.

I throw seed to the wind
and wind drops it on the desert.

The eighth year I spend planting corn;
I tend my fields all season.
After September's harvest I take it to the market.
The people of my village are too poor to buy it.

The ninth spring I make chicken feather headdresses,
plastic tom-toms and beaded belts.
I grow rich,
buy an old Ford,
drive to Chicago,
and get drunk
on welfare checks.

## AT THAT TIME

he left me in the Chevy
while he went hunting rabbits;
tracks across the damp meadow

      (the hound smell
      glows on the leather seat
      and its breath stains the glass

      dry corn stalks dance
      in a near field;
      cedar scents
      the woody afternoon;
      oak and ash
      finger November and my spine

      I hear his shot;
      mama didn't want me
      to have guns
      or make friends of hounds)

I was afraid of dead rabbits
and their bloody smell,
but he came from the woods
blood on his hands
and blood on his face;

I knew we'd live a little
longer . . . its blood was still
warm . . . despite mama

# THEY TELL ME I AM LOST

*For Lance Henson*

my feet are elms, roots in the earth
my heart is the hawk
my thought the arrow that rides
    the wind across the valley
my spirit eats with eagles on the mountain crag
    and clashes with the thunder
the grass is the breath of my flesh
    and the deer is the bone of my child
my toes dance on the drum
    in the light of the eyes of the old turtle

my chant is the wind
my chant is the muskrat
my chant is the seed
my chant is the tadpole
my chant is the grandfather
    and his many grandchildren
    sired in the frost of March
    and the summer noon of brown August
my chant is the field that turns with the sun
    and feeds the mice
    and the bear red berries and honey
my chant is the river
    that quenches the thirst of the sun
my chant is the woman who bore me
    and my blood and my flesh of tomorrow
my chant is the herb that heals
    and the moon that moves the tide
    and the wind that cleans the earth
        of old bones singing in the morning dust
my chant is the rabbit, skunk, heron

my chant is the red willow, the clay
    and the great pine that bulges the woods
    and the axe that fells the birch
    and the hand that breaks the corn from the stalk
    and waters the squash and catches stars
my chant is a blessing to the trout, beaver
    and a blessing to the young pheasant
        that warms my winter
my chant is the wolf in the dark
my chant is the crow flying against the sun
my chant is the sun
    sleeping on the back of the grass
        in marriage
my chant is the sun
    while there is sun I cannot be lost
my chant is the quaking of the earth
    angry and bold

although I hide in the thick forest
    or the deep pool of the slow river
    though I hide in a shack, a prison
    though I hide in a word, a law
    though I hide in a glass of beer
        or high on steel girders over the city
        or in the slums of that city
    though I hide in a mallard feather
        or the petals of the milkwort
        or a story told by my father

though there are eyes that do not see me
    and ears that do not hear my drum
    or hands that do not feel my wind
    and tongues which do not taste my blood

I am the shadow on the field
   the rain on the rock
   the snow on the wind
   the footprint on the water
   the vetch on the grave
I am the sweat on the boy
   the smile on the woman
   the paint on the man
I am the singer of songs
   and the hunter of fox
I am the glare on the sun
   the frost on the fruit
   the notch on the cedar
I am the foot on the golden snake
I am the foot on the silver snake
I am the tongue of the wind
   and the nourishment of grubs
I am the claw and the hoof and the shell
I am the stalk and the bloom and the pollen
I am the boulder on the rim of the hill
I am the sun and the moon
   the light and the dark
I am the shadow on the field

I am the string, the bow and the arrow

## WEJACK

groundhog
rumbled
in spring sun

waddles
down
last year's grass

not looking
for shadows
nor weathermen

just keeping safe
distance from dogs
yelping at the electric fence

not counting morning hours
nor drifting clouds
not even
sucker-minnows
plopping
on the eddy
of the black river

not even thinking
of his tail
prized by teenage hunters

he faced the sun
squarely
new iris shoots
wild onion
and entered the stream
to bathe off stale winter

## QUICKSAND

I cried into the quicksand creek
of childhood noon, poplar shadowed,
pools tickled by minnow bites

along the creek I lost the skin of new-born teeth,
and choked my teddy bear with wounded hands

along the bend of the stream I lost
the cry for milk, and sang instead
to rocks and thistles in the field

## IN COUNTRY LIGHT

Flesh tones streak the blue of frostbite;
cedar sky wheels, hawk over
expanse of salmon afternoon

a child cried because her mother
fell and broke a spider-arm
on river ice

shadows move, deer go;
close the door and stay by the fire;
listen, pine cones crackle
smell supper on the stove

## O WENDY, ARTHUR

One more night my blood
keeps sleep from the hard pillow.
Sula purrs at the foot of the bed
trying to sing me into dreams.
It doesn't work any more
than warm milk, valium, or exhaustion.
I sit here attempting poems
and fantasizing tours around the world,
wanting to feel your words,
desperate to talk, to tell
how spring climbed up with dawn
and iris bloomed the ridge of my arm,
and we three walked blackberry brambles
balancing on railroad tracks
through blue meadows. Could it be
that sleep defies some drift of happiness
that I can't measure, pin, explicate,
nor file away for the days when that sun
doesn't rise with wild flowers on my cheek.

This particular case of insomnia almost
feels good especially knowing you'll be here Wednesday.


Spring 1981

## FIFTY, FIFTY-ONE . . .

Snow on the hills
        (Wendy wouldn't call them mountains
        but laughed when I pointed)
with fifty birch bending
        into the horizon
grey in this grey morning
faceless except for the mountains
        for those fifty trees
I look for something to speak
        hawk, raven, ripple
of a sluggish stream scaring
        the snowed fields
Ice has silenced the birds, creek,
needled woodchucks, bears to sleep
wind doesn't own a voice, nor does it hear
        mine in this cold

If I can last this month
        perhaps spring will offer
a new reason to look at hills
        seeing them as mountains
and birch, feed robins raspberry seeds
plant saplings in old clearings
catch wind, let it sing
through my mouth and have no fear of the snow
        surely to fall next winter

March 1980, Vermont

# BLACKROBE: ISAAC JOGUES
## 1982

"Brother, we do not wish to destroy your religion
or take it from you. We want only to enjoy our
own."

—*Sagoyewatha (Red Jacket(*

## PEACEMAKER
*The Longhouse*

Protect
your house!
Lean
a pole
across
your door
so persons
not
entitled to enter
by right
shall not
enter
while you
are away
tending fields,
hunting,
fishing,
at ceremony.

I stutter
but the man
I send
will tell you
to lean a pole
and protect
your
house.

## AIIONWATHA
*(b. circa 1400)*

I have listened
and I will aid the stutterer
to unite the people
of this river country.
I will start with the Mohawk,
carry the word to Atotarho of the Onondaga,
advise him to take the bones
from the pot and water the pine.

I will travel and tell this
to both the younger brothers
and the elder brothers.
I will show them
the white roots of peace
as he has instructed.
We will mold a Nation.

## LITTLE PEOPLE
*Ceremony of the Dark Waters*

Three times he came to the woods
(once with his illness)
and stood above the quarry.
He didn't feed us purslane.
He went away without instructions.

He came a second time
(with the silver cross)
with beaver meat, but we did not eat.
He left without strawberries.

The third time he came
(with his book)
he brought raisins and brandy
but refused to throw them down to us.
We did not show him out of the woods.

The birds have ceased singing before his footsteps.

He will need to go to the story stone.




## WOLF
*Snakes*

Like the wind of a river
it weaves south from the snow
country leveling the woods,
swallowing all the rabbits
in the brush, trampling
the young berries. Its
silver skin defies the moon.

Tiger ribbon of cold flesh
ever-slithering north, a great
sturgeon in its jaw, its belly
obese with the hindquarter
of a spring fawn. The golden stripes,
brilliant, flaunt the sun.

## CAVELIER DE LA SALLE
*Explorer*

Two years before I birthed
he was there at Lake Superior
with Raymbault and a group of fur traders
converting Indians.

(That was Marquette's ruse.
That good father died of dysentery.
and left his bones at the river edge.
in 1676 an Ottawa hunting party
moved his remains in a birch bark box
and bore it in procession,
chanting funeral songs, to Michilimackinac.
He was the true counterpart of Jogues.)

But it was beaver, exploration,
colonization for the French crown
not the souls of infidels.

My purpose was to search out
the Mississippi
headwaters and expand
relentlessly.
we have all plotted our places in history.
Sincerely, Robert Cavelier.

## ROUEN, FRANCE

Madame! I go to New France.
The boat leaves tomorrow from Dieppe, the 2nd
Sunday after Easter. We dock
at Quebec. You do not know
how happy I am to learn that now
I will have the opportunity
of saving those lost souls for God.
Bless me and pray for me.
Thank you for the tin of tea.
It will be a comfort in the wilds.
Your very humble son, Isaac Jogues.


## AT SEA
*Letter to the Father Superior of the Jesuit Order in France*

Your High Reverence: I shall
manage this boat! This storm!
This fear! God is in my heart.
I lean upon the staff of Christ.

The sea swells like mountains.
The galley food is inedible.
The crew curses constantly.
Yet, I have few complaints.

God is in my heart,
and He will warm my chill.

The Hurons, *les hures*, I hardly dare
speak of the danger there is
of running oneself amongst
the improprieties of these
savages. I understand adultery
flourishes throughout their country.

Weakness is illness.

I hold to the cross,
Your obedient servant, Isaac Jogues.

## LES HURES
*Jogues' Journal*
*Three Rivers*

Naked, reddish-brown bodies
glisten like metal in the sunlight;
heavy, barbaric faces
with hooked noses and narrow-
slitted eyes; straight black hair
coiffed with feathers
of brilliant colors . . . green teal,
royal blue and canary yellow;
faces painted in lightning, color
of thunder; grunt instead of speak;
*les hures* pluck the hairs of the face.

It is exciting to be
here amongst these fetching
people . . . rogues which we Jesuits
will change into angels and saints.

# FIRST MEETING WITH KIOTSAETON

Like some marvelous bird
he stood on the river bank in plummage,
a feather headdress flaming in rainbow colors;
clothed in hide decorated
with beads and porcupine quills.
His neck, his arm hung heavily mailed
with brilliant wampum belts of shells.

He called me by my Huron name, Ondessonk*,
and passed a smoking pipe,
the calumet of peace.
I could not breathe for his resilience;
his air of royalty stunned my sensibilities.
His companions broke into song,
drum beat.
We exchanged gifts of food.

I believe his sincerity.
But what of his warriors
whose faces—on which I can discern
paint!—margin the woods.
What is his power over these men
who would as soon lift my hair
and chop off my thumb
as they would drink my brandy,
smoke our French tobacco.

I will not allow his honeyed words,
his venison or his pipe to halt
my journey south. I
represent the French crown!
and shall not be ambushed by trickery
nor denied my route,
nor fooled by the old man's white paint.

I pray for peace,
and safety,
but my determination
will circumvent all adversity.
I, son of God and priest
of Christ's blood.

*Ondessonk: Bird of Prey

## KIOSAETON

Ondessonk, through my lips
the Nation speaks. My words
are not malicious.
There is no evil in my heart
for you or your brothers
of the black robe.

My people have many war songs,
but we let them float
in the air as though canoes
drifting down the river.
The ground where we stand
does not pulse from the war dance,
nor does it thirst for your blood.

Here, take some corn and venison.
Eat now, rest. You are in safe
country with my people
who will respect your customs
and invite you into the lodge
if you maintain respect for ours.

## CARDINAL RICHELIEU

I sold my own jewels
to build forts at Sainte Marie.
I was impressed with the powerful strength
of the Iroquois. I had visions
of a New France bristling
with industry and commerce,
fur presses breaking, snapping
under the weight of beaver pelts.
My enthusiasm secured grants
from the public treasury, and I
dispatched my own soldiers
to the St. Lawrence to convoy
the Huron traders the full length
of the river. Saints be knighted!
My forces will not be driven out
of the country by Indians.
. . . I must replace the rings
I've sold in the open market.

## APPROACHING THE MOHAWK VILLAGE
*Jogues' Journal*

I enter the village
my silver cross held upright
though they told me to keep
it hidden in the folds of my robe.

Iroquois, give me your children,
your sick with fever and chill.
I have brought French raisins
to cure your influenza.
I have brought my beads and this cross
to cure your souls. I have
not brought death to your Nation.

Iroquois, give me your chieftains.
Give me your pride and arrogance.
Give me your wildness.
Give me your souls for God
and your sins for hell.


*Marginal Note*

Richly furred
beaver pelts
hang at the
entrance to
each
lodge.
Ahhhhhhh!

## BEAR

What do I want with his raisins!
or his blackrobe, his caudle of death.
And those beads or his mumbling.
There is blood on that cross he wears
around his neck, and even though the sun
strikes it and the moon glimmers
from its metal it has a power of
destruction. The beads are
the spittle of a snake. Didn't he come
from Huron country. His piety
is sickening. A weakling. His eye
is always either on pelts or dis-
tracted by the boys. What kind
of human is this who does not hunt
for his own food, but takes it from an old
woman's hand.
            If he would leave
the children alone . . . children make men . . .
I would not interfere with his
breathing.
            *Kwa-ah! Kwa-ah!* I'll wail
sadly across this village, and send
a runner to Atotarho. He will know what
to do with this blackrobe devil
when he raises that cross to the moon.

There is something strange in his step.

## AMONG THE MOHAWKS

Madame! At last! I'm in the village.
There is some fever here. Thankful to God
I have enough raisins. One woman has become
my friend, adopted me as a nephew. She will
protect me as I have enemies in the village.
Already she has freely given me food:
corn soup, dried venison . . . jerky they call it.
I can rest now awhile and pray.

Ambassador to the Mohawks!
A grand title for one so humble.
Madame will agree. I bring peace
to the breasts of these wildies.

Many beaver in the streams. The pelts
will make handsome chapeaux for our French
gentlemen and the grandees of China.
Salmon are fat. Game plentiful.
They seem to enjoy our brandy.
Your humble son, Isaac Jogues.

## VIMONT
*Father Superior of New France*

With the Cardinal's jewels
and demands we built the forts.
But will stockades strike at the root
of the evil? These barbarians
carry on war in the wanton manner,
ambush and torture, of Parthians.
The door to the south country
must be opened and danger repulsed.
The *Maguas*, as the Dutch are wont
to name them, must be pacified
or exterminated.
In the name of the Holy Father,
and the Son, and the Holy Ghost.

## ARENDT VAN CORLEAR
*Dutch Burgher*

He hovels in the attic
starving, near naked
after his escape from the *Maguas*
through the forest.
He trembles in prayer,
but crazed to leave for France
only to ready himself,
sharpen his holy weapons,
to return to the north villages.
His glassy eyes stare to heaven.
Jesus groans on his lips.

What should we make of this man-priest
whose sole concern, reason for
existence, is to die a saint.
Devotion is noble, but we must
make sure it does not
overwhelm good sense.

What I fear is his return
will so rile the *Maguas*
they will fire Renselaerwyck
and take *our* heads.
Ship him home to France . . .
immediately.

## THE PEOPLE OF THE FLINT

I openly refute their foolish tales
that the world was built on a turtle's back.
I try to reason the sun possesses no intelligence,
and that the sun is no god to man nor moose . . .
beautiful that it may be, needful to crops.
I cannot convince them that our Lord
is far more beautiful than this sun they worship.
And the absurd woman who fell from the sky
with the seeds of life under her fingernails,
and who, with the help of some rodent, brought
mud to the turtle's back and created earth with all
things growing . . . myths, untruths. Gently I shall
dispell this wicked and false belief.

And yet I pity the young children:
the girls picking berries in the long
grasses, the boys readying for war . . .
children who will not know the peace
of God and His kingdom. I'll persuade
them to the skirts of Mary, virgin mother
of Christ who bore her son's blood and pain
into miraculous ascension. Isaac Jogues, priest.

## WOLF 'AUNT'

I had the right to choose.
It is customary.
My own son was dead.
I needed to replace him
at both the lodge fire
and in my heart.
                    Women
need sons not only
for protection and bright
ornaments of quills and feathers.

I adopted Blackrobe . . .
before the people of the Bear
could strike a tomahawk
into his shaven head.


## BEAR

Our corn withers!

Worms bore through stalk and kernel.
We will starve
if this Blackrobe remains
in the village.

He possesses a small box
which contains his evil
potents and spells.

He has tampered with the corn
as his words have tampered
with the heads of our
foolish Wolf women.

His box must be split and emptied!

## WOLF 'AUNT'

They came to the lodge door
and called him by name.
*Blackrobe*, they called.
*Blackrobe, come out.*

Foolish and determined.
Obstinate, adamant.
Oh! He'll save these children
all right, but from the throne of his god.

I tried to persuade him
to return to the Hurons, his friends.
I told him not to carry that cross
when he walked alone in the village . . .

holding it, flaunting it in the faces
of both the chiefs and clan mothers.
I told him to stop mumbling
over the sick children,

that the duties of curing
belonged to our doctors
who have centuries of service
and the herbs to heal.

Would he listen! No!
At hearing of an illness
he would drop his bowl of food
and rush out into a blizzard

that cross before him, those beads
clanking on the wind.
I gave him a warm place to sleep,
and deer meat my brother killed.

With my own hands I sewed him moccasins.
I thought he would learn our ways.
All he learned was our language
so he could "speak to the people."

I threatened him
and told him the false-faces
would come when walking
in the woods, they would

bite his flesh and suck
out his spirit. Did he
listen! No, of course not.
Instead he made signs

over me, always smiling what others
thought a smirk, a leer, but he was
smiling. He was too dumb to smirk.
No, not dumb, but foolish.

I was positive that one day the Bear
would grow tired of his posturing,
that some doctor or other would become
jealous, fearful of his powers,

that a clan mother would envy his
living within my lodge,
that some boy would resent his stares,
and that a child would hear his

mumblings and scream out to his
uncle for help. I told him this
every morning of his life
and every night that predicted his death.

And finally they came to the door,
called him by name.
*Blackrobe*, they called.
*Blackrobe, come out!*

The moon was very beautiful that night.
Full and yellow. The shadows cast
were long, ominous.
The air was bright, sky blue.

He barely placed his foot on the earth
outside the lodge
when I heard a thump and I knew
his body crumpled under the club.

I will be searching
his bones for years . . .
bone by bone.

# BEAR

Had he the intelligence
to stay inside the lodge that night
he would still be studying his beads
and waving that cross in the air!
But he was stupid, stupid
in the way of all renegades:
stupid in the way all saints are.
He wanted to be martyred!
He'd sent his communiques
back to the French in Quebec,
and the Hurons; he'd prayed over
the sick . . . to the fury of our own
doctors; he mumbled to our children,
swathed them with enough fur
to choke out their breath . . .
he could not bear the sight
of naked flesh, nor two people
coupling in the shadows of the lodge.
Chastity, he called, chastity!
These foreign words
stung many a full-bodied
male and female. Yet, he stared
at the young boys swimming nude
in the river. And flew to make signs
over their heads.
                    It was not so much
that we were sure an army
would follow his step through the woods
. . . we knew the Frenchmen were
ambitious, and the Dutch conniving
thieves coming from the south . . .
it was his preaching,
his determined wish to change,
his power to invoke change,
his power to strike out a past
that has taken centuries to build,
and his dark powers culled
from a remote land and godhead
we people feared and mistrusted.

Besides that, I didn't like
the hook of his nose and that cross
he thrust into my teeth and his
whiny breath on my bare arm.
But most his box!

We gave him sanctuary.
We extended all the hospitality
necessary to carry out the law
and to satisfy the demands
of the Seneca. His aunt . . . hah!
his aunt fed him meat her brother
took down, and squash she labored
hot summers to grow. She picked
him berries and cut sweetgrass
to scent his pillow. She probably
nourished his lust, or gave him
her daughter's loins. (Yet I fear
he abstained, refused that pleasure
while staring at the nude boys playing games.)

The moon was ripe as melons.
Cedar scented the night air.
White pine shimmered in the light.
A hawk had passed over the village
that afternoon, and a snapping
turtle came from the river mud.
There was a smell of parched corn
emanating from a lodge. I told
the men to stay at home
with the women and children.
I told the doctors to prepare
a ceremony, and the soldiers
to sharpen the points of their spears.

With two friends I slipped through
the quiet of the village . . . not even
the dogs stirred in their lazy sleep.
We approached his aunt's house
and called out to him. I could hear
her arguments . . . that the Seneca
would come. I knew, however, he would
step out into the darkness.

We spoke briefly, a last
warning for his spirit's flight.
Then the clubs rained upon his head.
Still holding his cross out to us
he sank to the earth, the cross
scraped the flesh of my thigh
and his blood spurted onto my moccasin.

I left my two companions to deal
with his young friend. I
immediately returned to my lodge
and the doctors purged my flesh
with burning cedar smoke, and
awaited the Seneca runners.

I don't know what they did
to his corpse. His old aunt
says she still finds his
bones along the creek bed.
His head was impaled upon
the highest pole of the village stockade.

## OCTOBER 18, 1646
*Thursday*

Madame, I am thirty-nine years old.
My fingers bleed where
old women have chewed the nails.
My feet swell from long hikes
and the snap of dogs' teeth.

They say now that I must
be sacrificed to placate
spirits which have been offended.
The chiefs and the clans
are in council to argue

the will of this Nation.
Spit dries on my cheek.
Madame, your humble son
in Christ and in death,
Isaac Jogues.

# HIS VISIONS

*1.*
Revelation

*'Exaudita est oratio tua;*
*fiet tibi sicut a me petisti.*
*Comfortare et esto robustus.'*

*2.*
At the death of Rene Goupil

If I am to die
let it be swift. If I
am to die for Christ
and my heavenly Father, let it be clean.

My aunt says I am foolish.
I should wait for the chiefs'
decision, and that the Seneca
are friendly towards me as well
as the Wolf and Turtle people.
Perhaps!

Rene, and now Jean, my boon companions,
counseled to remain here . . . one to die
and the other to stay in safety
in the lodge by the fire
where we should be safe. Safe!
Safe from my duty to preach,
to heal, to surrender to God
what is God's. I must accept
the Bear's invitation to the feast.
Now, my only fear is for the life
of young Jean de la Lande who
will perish once my head
rolls on the ground.

What greater sacrifice can I
make for God and the salvation
of these brothers who I shall
and must lead to God.

No, good woman, I will attend the feast.
No, kind Jean, I will respond to the Bear's call.
I will martyr my blood
for the cause of God and even though
I am an alien in this land
I will example my life for Jean
and for these innocents
who are in need of God's love,
Yes, if I am to die let it be swift.


*"Thy Prayer is heard. Be it done to thee as though first asked. Be comforted, be of strong heart."


## JEAN DE LA LANDE
### His Companion

His life has been a reverence,
a flight of birds,
it has been a celebration.
A bouquet of his words
has colored my own vocation.
His work's the joy of meadowlarks.
I am prejudiced
in my respect for his hem.

I wade my life in the flow of his blood,
and seek his corpse in the village streets
where my veins will soon nourish the grass,
the wild purslane we ate along our way.

Father Jogues, we can't have been wrong
to have entered these woods, or has
our fervor rendered us into hell!

## BEAR

The French are here in large
numbers. They demand retribution,
but will settle for beaver pelts,
however, and an opened gate to the Mohawk
Valley. Claim they will back us
in a fight with the Dutch, or English.
They don't give a damn for their
martyr, the blackrobe, whose bones
the dogs gnaw before their eyes.

All men suffer the same disease.

They will take the mountains,
and probably the valley rivers.
They aren't interested
in burying his bones.

My men enjoy their brandy.

# THE FRENCH INFORMAL REPORT

We've lost another. With his idiotic
pouch of raisins he went into Mohawk
villages to cure influenza and save
their souls. He was told to wear buckskin,
to be silent, not to raise his cross.

These priests cannot be trusted
to carry out an order.

Oh! he was a good man, pious, devout,
of good cheer, selfless, respected.
That's all true. Ungrudgingly
he tramped the wilds by foot or canoe;
survived privation, torture; overcame
whatever adversity: illness, hunger, lust.

But he was a fool. Should have stayed
in France with the other saints.
He's foiled our plans. The Dutch laugh
in our face, and the English frigates
approach New Amsterdam harbor, their guns
aimed, their greed as large as everyone's.
Beaver is something to squabble about.

Isaac Jogues, get thee to a priory.
Raise turnips within the cloister's walls.
Eat your raisins.
                    The scouting party
found few bones to bury. The Mohawks
are distressed. They dance all night.


*Marginal Note*

Remember
to send
more brandy
for the savages.
They guzzle
with gusto.

## BEAR

I honor his courage,
and the devotion to his friend.

But I sleep easier knowing
their heads top the posts . . .
the hollow sockets of their eyes
a warning to those who might follow.

It is that very courage, bravery
in men that I fear the most.

# HOANTTENIATE
*Jogues' Adopted 'Wolf Brother'*

I trembled
when his warm hand touched
my bare shoulder, when his solemn eyes
sought my furtive glance.

I will never forget the soft sounds
of his skirt crossing the grass,
nor his exclamations
at the sight of deer in the woods.

Nor will I ever forget his muffled cry
when the club split his head
and the spurts of blood hissed
through the snakes of his hair.

I cannot bring my eyes to stare
into the river waters now
mingling with his blood. The fish
nibble pieces of his flesh.

(I will miss the touch of his fingers
and his whispering through the corn fields
while reading his book, and the sweet
raisins he offered the boys and myself.)

## TEKAKWITHA (KATERI)
*"Lily of the Mowhawks"*
*1656-1680*

The hands which hold the silver beads
will never know the hoe, seeds of squash
or beans, or corn nor the dirt of their womb.
The lips that kiss the cross of Christ,
this heart which homes the spirit of God,
this flesh which shall shortly fade
will know the habit of silence, the caul of joy.
I give His priests the blood of my veins,
and prayer which flutters like songs
of meadow hummingbirds; I give my morning light,
the labor of my evening knees at work in prayer.

Though I am driven from the village by my own people
to race before wolves, bed with vipers, sleep
under the crust of snow, know painful hunger . . .
I shall be safe and warm and satiated
with food of the Holy Ghost, the blessed
Sacrament of the Eucharist in communion.
I shall atone for the sins of my people,
and for my own sins of ignorance and blasphemy.
My zeal will obtain penance and my spirit peace.

Friend, be kind, accept this whip.
Like winter wind let its leather thongs
scream through the air and strike my flesh.
Like juice of the raspberry blood shall
trickle from my shoulder blades, my arms.
Each Sunday of the week I shall embrace purity.

I walk in veils and know paradise.

## ARONIATEKA
*(c. 1680-1755)* ˮ

The Rev. Mister Jonathan Edwards
persuaded me to Christianity;
taught my hands to work the plow.

...

I am in my 70th year now.
Today we war the French.
I know from my dream last night
I shall not survive this battle.
As I told Colonel Williams:
if my warriors are to fight,
they are too few;
if they are to die,
they are too many.

We defeated the French
at Lake George today.
Their rags return to Three
Rivers and Quebec.

...

My wife has taken my broken bones
to the mountains where the pine
stretching toward the sky-world
and the howling wolves will guard
the remnants of Aroniateka,
or, as you have renamed me,
Hendrick.

## TURTLE

They are here now
in blackrobes and hoods;

they walk through the forest
whispering words from a book;

their hair cut short, noses
tight, eyes sharp as a hawk.

One day they will come off the river
with hair as long as our own,

a feather attached loosely,
wearing buckskin shirts

and squash blossom ornaments
about their throats, hanging

on naked chests. You can tell . . .
some have already begun to smoke

our sumac, bathe, and
speak with the holy men.

One day they will come so thick
we will need to chase them off

with brooms and close the doors
of the lodges as though a pole

stood sentinel at the entrance
and the village was empty.

Someday they will come
to learn . . . not to teach.

The blackrobes have many feet
beneath their long skirts.

## ROKWAHO
### 1978

He dropped names on the land . . .
ticks sucking the earth . . .
De Feriet, LeRay, Herrick,
and Brown, Chaumont, Malone, Pulaski.
Out of his black robe came Kraft,
feedmills, blight, Benson Mines.
From his prayers flowed death
of salmon and trout in mercury pools.
From letters home to his
mother settlers followed
soldiers behind hooded priests.

In his pouch he carried raisins
to cure the influenza his people
brought to the shores of the lake.
His raisins have not flourished
though his influenza remains
raging like a torrential river
flooding the banks, swallowing
fields and woods and whatever
animal standing in the way.


. . .
My hair and tongue are cut!

# THE MAMA POEMS
## 1984

". . . Right-handed Twin came naturally from his
mother, the daughter, impregnated by the West
Wind, of Sky-woman. But his brother, Left-
handed Twin, impatiently sprang early from his
mother's armpit and killed her from his unnatural
escape from her body."

*—from the Mohawk version
of the Iroquois creation story*

# 1911

Those fields and orchards. Barns hot with swallow flight. Your father's yellow rose bush circling the drive to the old homestead leaning into greyness, yet standing sturdy in the laughter of seven young girls ginghamed to the throat, swollen in wool though June stepped sprightly across fields and into berries brightening the meadows under larks and thrushes, pheasants fanning brush through woods of day lilies late to spring early to summer while your mama stood on the long front porch rotting beneath her feet screaming to the afternoon as her hands rose from wrinkled apron to hair whisking about her oval face shrouded in spots of anger that her seven daughters played on the neighbor's lawn.

The apple tree, translucent, yellowing the hour, ridiculous in its spiney, wobbly erection, tended with fervent hands by "pa," arching in birth of leaf and blossom, scenting the heavy air as wisteria weights the breeze; the apple for teeth, for sauce, for jack, for pie; the apple, symbol to your "pa" what has been and can be in its aging bend with no new branches struggling through winter snows to break open spring. Disappointment that young Charles died a babe. The apple, shade to chickens and gobblers; the apple where your mama threw out the coffee grinds, cabbage leaves, eggshells, wet corncobs.

We loved it. Your grandma, my grandpa, you, us. (Four years ago, the house depleted in a hunter's ruin, old boards nailless from greed, old walls stripped of paper, not even a dented bedpot left in the rubble. The house down about the heads of the ghosts, crumbled into the spring cellar where brine once kept pork and pickles, where carrots and squash stayed bright and crisp. And all the voices, the voices of birth, and the wails of death, and the joy of holiday . . . came tumbling down.)

Oh! Mama, there was seldom happiness there. But beauty stood its ground. The earth shuddered, the fields, the orchards now bitter to the touch and the taste, the chicory, the bats of evening, the pitchers of ginger-beer, iced melon. No, there was never happiness there while your "pa" spent his winter nights reading from the Bible in the barn, his place, allocated by your mama who would never allow his pipe in the parlor, your dirty stockings on the bedroom floor. Girls were raised to work, to carry water for the laundry, wash dishes, scrub floors, shake the tick in the morning wind, scythe the grasses, and bend, bend, forever bend in the berry fields where you bled profusely on the fruit. Your face and gingham spotted with your first knowledge, your first lesson. You were never able to wash the blood away. It stuck, hard and dark to your cheek, your hands. And you cried in the fields where iris brightened the morning still heavy with dew and night-fear, where hawks gleaned the grain of mice and woodchucks, where the mirage of old women, hideous in masks, came to pinch your arm and whisper terrible tales into your ear. Beware of the night, the shade and the wind that comes out of the west. Beware of the breath. Let me touch your hair. And it turned white. You were a child, and your hair turned white at the washer wringer. You screamed and the hideous old woman laughed a cackle that frightened the cocks crowing to the hens. And your mama spanked and took away the dessert from supper, a dish of gooseberry sauce. You wept in bed from all sorts of pain. Pain that would never leave your breast, your breast little and as pretty as a flower bud, a little fist that would open to mouths you never really learned to comprehend.

And the blood stayed on your cheek. It was there last month in the coffin. Brilliant in its birthmark. Not even my kiss washed it away. But the fields remain though barren without cow, a blind horse, a child's print. The fields, the land reeking with ghosts and voices gurgling the temper of the times. Deplete. Fields returning to scrub woods. And so it should be.

## LITTLE VOICES

We live in a quarry
with walls we cannot climb,
without meat, though we know
many stories and raise
berries on the sandy floor.

A ragged boy came to our woods . . .
to shoot squirrels for his
mother's empty pot;
his lazy uncles would not
pick up the bow and arrows.

He shared his game.
We kept the boy with us
four days, and when he left
he took vines and all
the stories we had to tell.

When he arrived home
his village had moved.
He found his mother old and sick
and his uncles dead from hunger,
but he carried wild strawberries,

and when his mother drank
the juice and had heard the tales
he learned from us
she rose from her bed
well and strong and spread her son's

adventure to all people.
Now, in June,
the people have berries
to pick and juice to drink
when someone is sick;

now we receive game to eat
when a hunter passes through
the woods, and pauses
above the quarry.
Our fires are always lit.

# COMING TO AN UNDERSTANDING

You must have been a girl . . .
before you became my mother.


...

Remember your father's rose
bush circling the drive
where turkeys slept beneath
yellow petals in the raging sun;
remember him reading his Bible
in the barn, smoking his pipe
his wife would not allow in her parlor.
I'm sure you picked apples.


...

There is little I know.
I guess you never dreamed,
nor caught a thumb in a turtle's snap,
nor chased butterflies nor were,
in turn, chased by the bull
snorting in childhood meadows.


...

How can I continue without
knowing, without stopping
the blood from your cut finger,
licking your batter bowl, choking.

# SOMETIMES . . . INJUSTICE

The day I was born my father bought me a .22.
A year later my mother traded it for a violin.
Ten years later my big sister traded that
for a guitar, and gave it to her boyfriend . . .
who sold it.

Now you know why I never learned to hunt,
or learned how to play a musical instrument,
or became a Wall St. broker.


# MAMA FAILED TO KILL THE RAT . . .

Mama failed to kill the rat
when it ran across my bed
that November my father tore the wall away
building the new addition to the house.
Snow seeped in, and not only snow:
raccoon thought it a good winter place;
squirrel cached hickory nuts.
Mama stood in the doorway
with a lamp in her grip
and told me not to move.

Since then rodents, mice have
always meant change to me, dead
or alive; a different course.

When corn leans, chestnuts fall;
when neighbors take in the screens
and fishermen put away
hooks and poles, late autumn,
I don't sleep so very well,
but still see Mama in the doorway
in the light of that kerosene flame
her face contorted in the mask
of chilled horror.

Mice have always meant change to me.
I hear rats gnawing the floor.

## INHERITANCE

Your pleasure was running,
to be on the go, downtown
to try on hats where you got lice once
and brought them home to us.
When you learned to drive
his Chevy you drove us to Canada.
They wouldn't let you cross the bridge
President Roosevelt built for us
because you weren't a citizen
of these United States.

Your running taught me how to run.
I keep Greyhound rich.
However, I learned
from your embarrassment never
to try on hats or cross bridges
into lands where I am not wanted.

## WAKE

In coffin light
I played with cobwebs . . .
hammock strung from corner
to corner knowing she slept
the winter day and winter cold
through the baked salmon supper,
whiskey drunk behind the barn,
the arrival of old aunts
and young cousins

I remember the white of her hair
bunned and hidden behind
the waxened face shorn of breath;
they had her clench a blue rosary
which brought meadows to her cheeks
and swallows to her lips
sealed then and finally with paraffin

Women climbed the stairs
with sleeping children in their arms,
others carried bowls of succotash
to tables crowded with hunger
as men sang songs;
I touched her stiffness with my lips:
there was music in her hands
and I would hear their stories

## THE LAST WORD
### (In memory of my Father)

He was an ornery cuss,
bull-headed as a Hereford,
sensitive as a sitting hen.

No doubt he gave you a rough time,
probably whacked you once or twice.
(I remember taking the broom to him,
and that finished our affair for life.)
He was known to take a glass of beer,
and I've heard it said he'd pinch
a waitress' buttocks, never refused a bed.
He taught you how to drive his car
and promptly took the Ford away.
He'd buy you a new dress and grumbled
if you wore it. He even upbraided you
for buying a pound of butter
at fifteen cents a pound.
One year he furiously threw
the Christmas tree down the cellar stairs
when he couldn't nudge the lights to blink.
After he bought the radio
he never went to Mass,
but never missed a funeral.
He dressed in tailor-made suits
and wore white shirts you pressed.
Monday through Thursday he was a gentle man,
coy as a kitten, soft as a rabbit.
He showed his colors Friday nights
when we kids went through his pockets
for dimes and nickles which rolled
from his pants along the kitchen floor.

But he paid Agnes' way to Missouri
and gave Mary a husband to keep
'til death did them part, and he got me
out of trouble as fast as I got in.
Even after the divorce he made payments
on your insurance policy.

                                    He died.
The very last word he said was,"Doris."

144

# PICKING BLACKBERRIES

Monday sun slants across the bush,
August brushes your hair in wind
off Lake Ontario; the watch
ticks at your wrist while the kids
squabble over who has the larger can,
the most berries, the blackest tongue.

Mrs. Anthony telling
stories in your ear
over berries meant for pie
to please your man
that might come tonight . . .
"the way to a man's heart
is through his belly."
You know that is a lie.

Your qualities were never baking,
but when you rolled up the sleeves
and baited your own hook,
or cleaned a mess of trout
or string of November rabbits
even when we demanded you darn
socks or heal blisters, fight
a cold . . . you spent years pleasing
what was not to be pleased,
darning where there were no holes,
picking berries more to gossip
with Mrs. Anthony than for pies,
forgetting teeth
needed tending, taking up
a glass of water in the dark
when Mary cried in fever,
or sitting at the winter window
watching snow in tears
telling us when he will come,
when he will go with no
understanding of what love is.

There's a plastic plant on his grave.
Yours is marked, name
chisled into stone, the fence
around erected, prayer cards
about ready to be printed,
and still you have no idea
of what picking blackberries
was all about, you would bend
an ear to Mrs. Anthony
telling stories . . .
"the way to a man's heart
is through his stomach."

The end of the week, rain every day;
the lake is black in storm, Agnes' kids
are just about all married. You placed
the old watch in the dresser drawer,
and write letters to the family saying
how sorry you are to have missed sending
Christmas presents this year, and that
Mary's arthritis is getting worse.

. . .

Sparrows and wrens pick the blackberries.

146

# ON THE STATEN ISLAND FERRY

You brought me here when I was ten.

...

A friend suggested I write
a novel of how I wanted to push
you off the ferry into the wake . . .
fall like Sky-woman fell from the old world.
My friend said impatience cured
curiousity, but I don't think novels
cure pain nor intention of guilt.

This morning the sun hangs
in the eastern sky and the moon
sits in the west. They eye each other,
jealous siblings never
willing to share a dandelion
nor rib of venison. As I could not do
without a mother we cannot do
without their argument.
They'll continue contesting
on such mornings as this, and I
will continue pleased that you
had not been swallowed in the ferry's wake.


...

My father took me home again.

JOSHUA CLARK
*Three Mile Bay, N.Y.*
*July 1979*

*I*

name stained in colored glass
on the Baptist window erected
in the English spirit of your fervor

let me tell you, Pastor Joshua,
great-great-great grandfather,
bred in the clover spring of 1802,
bed to Sybil, sire of Mary
sire to the stones of this
seedy cemetery bloody from veins
opened to the summer breeze,
let me tell you, Joshua,
even your bones are dust.
the headstone chips in the sun
white asters climb
moisture of the grasses
wending across your name

yes, let me tell you, Joshua Clark,
your great-grandson married
the Seneca girl whose father's land
you stole, and his brother drunk
in the velvet parlor lifted cup
by cup the earth to the tavern keeper's smile
yes, my grandfather paid it away, too,
acre by acre to maids that came to dust
his wife's music room and to hired hands
who plowed his father's fields
until only your church and cemetery plot
were left and safe from their foolishness

Joshua, the apple trees have claimed
the house, sumac fill the cellar bins,
the stone foundations bed mice
and snakes prowl your yellow roses
where once you sat in the shade, counting souls
drinking ginger-beer
eyeing the westerly sun
black with barn swallows
your woods are cleared, hickory axed;
there is not a single creek
in those meadows, even bats
and hawks have fled;
your blood has thinned into a trickle . . .
I claim very little and pass nothing on . . .
not a drop to any vein.


your siring is finished, deeds done
and accomplishments or not only a name
remains penned into an old family Bible
and stained in glass, purple and green
of a church no one visits
but skunks and black spiders;
there are enough babies squawking anyway.

*II*

you were a strong man, strong as the elms
which once reared over the front lawn
and the white pine which fenced the fruit
orchard where ginghamed Sybil plucked
sweet cherry and damson plum
and teased your loins with her pretty English face
her thin ankle and narrow waist;
you were a strong man in the blood
your sap ran April
and you fathered our centuries, our wars
our treacheries, our lies,
our disappointing lives, loves; your fingers
coiled the rope which bound and trussed us all
on the hanging tree, the roots of our feet
dangling over the earth wet with blood
rockets exploding about our ears
deaf and blind as your drunken grandson
to the waste of blackberry brambles
and the loud gnawing of rats in the sweat
of your goose down mattress where Sybil birthed
Mary and all the dawns of your hairy thighs

old cats purr on the supper table
of cold beef; goats munch clean
meadows in the twilight of
birch bending to the rainbows of mornings past.

*III*

Patty-Lyn and Craig
never read your epitaph,
nor knelt in your Baptist church nor tested
Sybil's plum preserves, nor haven't
the slightest thought that Ely Parker
was a great Seneca General who had little to do
with your Baptist God;
hands were unfinned, unwebbed for tools
to preserve and beget and protect
all that's beautiful in trout and mallard
all which is remarkable in fire and ice
all which is noble in blood and loin
all which births and dies
in the raging sunset, of dawn;

this half-blood Mohawk condemns your church
to ash and though I would not tamper with the earth
which holds your dust I would chip the stone
flake by flake that heralds your name and deeds
but carry pails of fresh water to the green cedar
rooting in your family plot where my bones
refuse to lay coiled and pithed in the womb
of a tribe which has neither nation nor reason nor drum

my father claims my blood
and sired in the shadow of a turtle my growls
echo in the mountain woods where a bear climbs down
rocks to walk across your grave to leave its prints
upon the summer dust and pauses to sniff a wild hyssop
and break open a beehive for the honey of the years
and smack its lips on red currants

old cats should be wild and feed on field mice.
Joshua, I've nearly lost the essence of your name
and cannot hear the murmur of your time.
I stand throwing rocks at the stained glass
of your fervor knowing time ceases with the crash
the tinkle of the stones striking glass,
and all our blood between the installation
and the retribution has vaporized into the bite
of a single mosquito sucking my arm
in the summer breeze of this seedy cemetery

now sleep

# MISBEGOTTEN SONNET

There's not much sense to love,
nor much understanding . . . mainly
for kids who can't imagine why you'd
give up one man for another.

We change loves as wolves shed
winter fur for spring weather.
We change one face for another
without having learned the first.

Divorce is final, walls
between understanding.
It solves nothing;
a clean apron over a dirty dress.

## 1978

You've had your soldier thirty years.
He's fought many wars
all at your kitchen table
with his face in the green pea soup,
his flesh cold as a pickled egg.
His shriveled dreams
an olive on a pick.

Not all soldiers return
from war; they thrill to battle
and mutilation.
We could find excuses.
I, for one, refuse to look,
to lift the tablecloth in search
of what might have been a man.

# CALENDAR

Winter's count is slower:
pine breathing, hawk sighted on an elm,
barn leaning, a late call to Wendy
suffering flu with Arthur.
Mama aging and vague.

Why do we count, keep tally
moon after moon when nothing much
changes, happens, progresses.
We move into light and shadow,
collect time like rings, old pennies,
feathers; we sweep fallen hair
off the shoulder, sit closer to the t.v.
with the cat and memories.

Spring tells the count:
Mary's cherry tree snapped in half
by winter's weight; Aunt Jennie curled
tighter into age; the neighbor's wife
fat again with child; fewer birds sing.

# BLACK RIVER—SUMMER 1981

*For Patti-Lyn*

The evening river carries no sound . . .
not the bark of this fox whose skull
weights my hand,
nor the wind of this hawk
feather tucked into the buttonhole of my shirt.

Rivers grumble and hiss and gurgle;
they roar and sing lullabies;
rivers rage and flow and dance
like unseen wind;
in the dark they carry the eyes
of stars and footprints of deer.

> I have slept on your arm,
> dawn sweetening my mouth,
> stiff in limb
> and rose to your morning song.

> I have watched geese fly over,
> eels slither downstream,
> bullheads defy rapids,
> spiders ripple waves
> in trapped inlets along the shore,
> fireflies light paths
> from murky banks
> to mysterious islands
> where witches live.

> I have studied your waters:

> Daydreamed my watch to listen,
> to feel your tremble,
> to learn your summer,
> touch your winter,
> and be content.

## TELEPHONE CALL

He's going to Alaska
to pick tulips this time.

You're there?
I've been dialing wrong numbers.

I fell the other day.
Hurt my back. My liver pains.

No, I eat, I say I eat.
He cooked a t.v. dinner
and told me I was strong enough
to wash the supper dishes.
My bones ache.

This time he's going to pick tulips.
Where? Well, maybe it is
the lilac festival in Rochester.
I don't know why he wants to go to Alaska.
Said I fell on purpose so he couldn't go.
I don't care where he goes.

Mary works hard making pies and boiling stews
for those priests. Her cat is dead. Killed
on the highway. Found it in a heap of blood
in the snow. She's lonely. They gave her a dog .
It won't stay home either.

Jennie's thin. Mere bones,
but she stays on the road selling Avon.

No, I never hear from Agnes.
She's one daughter I've lost, I guess.

Oh! yes. My nurse comes,
but hasn't been here for two weeks.
I cleaned all my house before
the cleaning woman came. Couldn't
have her find it dirty.

Why does he want to go to Alaska to pick tulips?
Well, good night. Write.

## MAMA
*For Helene*
*On Her 30th Birthday*

The runt of the litter
of seven little girls.

I don't want to spend
too much time on the idea
of how deprived you were.
There is already too much
pity in this world,
nor get saccharine about you
rocking me to sleep in your arms
and baking bread in a hot oven,
or breaking your back
in a field of blueberries.
Nor remind you of how you favored
my sister, or denied me for the man
whose puke you've cleaned up for years.
I've pretty much forgotten that.
However, I doubt we ever forgive.
There's enough distance now
to separate fact from fiction
and to remind myself
you were/are a woman . . .
capable of being human . . .
your skin wrinkles as does mine,
your flesh withers.
We're of the same cut;
the same cotton cloth.
I knew your wet nipples;
you knew my sharp teething.

Mama, they called
very late the other night.
Woke me up at 3 a.m.
What could I say at such an hour,
what could I do.
I couldn't rock you in my arms,
nor stuff you into a tote bag
and ride Greyhound to California
where you'd be safe in the sun.
Nor could I convince them
that a woman is not a Ford,
that when it stops running
you take it to the junkyard
and sell it for used parts.
They wouldn't buy that.

      Mama we're all runts.

Eventually we'll all
be placed away from ourselves
where we can't harm
ourselves; where the tough
and strong won't need to worry
nor interrupt the baseball game
to check if we're all right
lighting the kitchen stove.

Mama, shake your head.
Bite the first hand that puts
a finger on your arm.

The moon is rising on the woods.
The apples ripen.
Some crazy hound howls down the road.
The neighbors watch "All
in the Family"
while the kid stands in the dark
of the stairwell crying
for a glass of Coke.
Cops crawl through the night
looking for trouble to start.
Joe St. Louis is drunk again.
One day he'll freeze in the snow
on the way home from the bar.

Mama, shake your head.
It's up to you to fight.
That place is full to the rafters
with folks that wouldn't bite,
I know, Mama, I was there . . .
remember.

# DECEMBER

Set up the drum.
Winter's on the creek.

Dark men sit in dark kitchens.
Words move in the air.
A neighbor is sick.
Needs prayer.

Women thaw frozen
strawberries.

In the dark . . . a drum.

> Kids hang out
> eating burgers
> at McDonald's.
> The Williams boy
> is drunk

Set up the drum.

Berries thaw,
are crushed,
fingers stained, and tongues.


Set up the drum
A neighbor is sick.
Say a prayer.
Dark men sit in dark kitchens.

Wind rattles the moon.

## MAY 15, 1982
### THREE MILE BAY, NEW YORK

I've failed often; this was my worst failure.

They took the red casket from the winter vault
while I was riding Greyhound in California.
No excuse.

It was a lovely day Aunt Ruth wrote.
Spring and lilac. Dandelions. Blue sky, a few clouds,
a fishing boat in the bay. Perfect.

                                        Not many there:
Mary, Ruth and Jennie, and Martin hobbling on his
new cane. Mary said he ordered a nice headstone,
and showed stress signs of his loneliness, regret,
shame for the abuse of years. Too late. I don't know
if a preacher was there. It wouldn't revive you,
nor ease pain you knew in your depths.

I used to believe in the powers of death.
Until you died.
It was the last belief.
I believe in echoes now,
in earth that holds you. I believe in a bird,
its flight, though I'm not sure which one, hawk
or seagull; the cedar near your grave, and the lake
not far away that you feared from childhood.
Summer is here on the chicory, harvest is next,
then winter which chilled, always, your arms.
I believe in seasons, time, too, I'd suppose.
There isn't much between mewl and rattle . . .
an occasional laugh at some human joke,
and more hurt than the human heart can bear;
disappointment, and the terrible lack of love.
I won't tally the balance sheet.

                                        I miss you.
I'm sorry I failed. This time I can't say
I won't do it again, because I probably would.

You might be happy now. You're where you wanted to be...
in the Bay under the cedar near your father
whom you loved. He was a good man you always said.
Perhaps the only man who was kind.

160

                                        I'm saccharine.
I don't mean to be. Dying isn't a ruined dinner.
I mean to be truthful, sincere, dispassionate . . .
which is difficult . . . forthright. I mean
to remember you as I ride the Greyhound in the dark,
or pick berries, or stroke my cat, or burn rice.
I'm not good at elegies . . . not even yours, my mother,
condolences, buying plants, telephoning, saying
thank you . . . as I wasn't good at kissing cheeks, or
showing up for supper on time. But you lied
for me then . . . as you lied for all your men.
Perhaps you'll lie again for me now that I fail.

# REVERBERATION

A north wind heard is heard always.
Drums reverberate like circles of a disturbed pool
into an incomprehensible time;
the banging of the drum does not stop
once thumped in the ceremony of life.

How can I explain optical illusion.
Can I cut her heart muscle into tiny pieces,
her brain, and set these pieces down on paper,
or in the palm of my hand. Memory weeds chaff.
Attempting to recreate the woman she was
through jottings of conversations, hand movements,
facial expressions, thought pattern, she
becomes a quirk of the imagination.
There remains a strong need in the blood,
strong in the verb orphaned in loneness,
roots pulled out by the hair. Are lips
still too close to nipple and breath.
Will she also come and sit at midnight.

I'll chatter with shadows filtering rooms,
watch the rocking chair rock, smell an apple pie
bubbling in a cold oven, hear a tea cup smash
on the floor of a vacant kitchen, or hear whispers
in the parlor where there are no voices.

They stay where they are wanted . . .

Home. To fields and woods. To the frightening river I shied and the hills my horse cropped early June mornings. The fence that tore my calf when Lightning panicked and took me over the fence and cliff. The scar remains indelibly creased on the flesh. It is for this reason I remember, and I remember nearly everything.

I etch on the walls of my study. Hawk's feathers, a swallow's nest, sweetgrass, pebbles, and old boards that collect dust each time the imaginary tick sucks blood from behind my ear. I carry out yellowed snapshots. Grandpa leading his white horse to the trough. You big with Mary, Agnes in your arms . . . myself not the twinkle of your wildest thought, or fear. You loved photographs. Your walls crawled with them . . . Martin, in war uniform proudly riding a tank, Pat in his Marine blues; Mary, young and beautiful, her eyes flashing. Agnes dressed in her Catholic uniform from the Conservatory. Myself, a snip of adolescent confidence. A known lie. Facade. They all wore facades. And you believed in them. It was all you had to believe. Photos that left old dust marks on the walls when he took them down and threw your dreams into the garbage. You sat night after night with the album by your side on the couch usually with your arthritic hand touching your babies, what you thought were your loved ones. (Do you know my father secretly carried your snap in his pocket until he died?) Is life merely a photograph? For some. For you.

He let you die alone. He told no one. Deprived. Depleted like your old homestead. The hunter took the kill and left you a crumble of old bones like boards, broken windowpanes. You went into death without a yellow rose from your father's circle. Denied. Your spirit as thin and transparent as saran. You hated cold. And you were freezing. February. And all your hopes lay in tubes and vials. I can see you spitting up your hospital supper. I can hear you say, I must lose weight, though you weighed barely eighty pounds. Eighty pounds of disappointment and hurt. He allowed you to die alone. The man you feigned adoration for, the man whose puke soiled your age, whose vomit of cheap sweet wine you bent and cleaned. OH! Mama, he didn't love you. He didn't even like your cooking. You became a drag on his cane. You were his cane and his hammer and his claw. You became everything despicable to him. Until now. Now that you are a part of the root of that cedar on your father's grave next to you. Now he remembers how beautiful your face had been and how straight your back, and firm your breast, how sweet your mouth. Now he touches reality. His right foot is about to step into shadow. You are revenged. Not that you probably want to be. But I want you to be revenged . . . for everything. Even my own father, who was as cruel as his love could be, as any love, as all love can be. Even though he carried your snapshot into the rattle of his death.

We're still reaching for an understanding. Of so many things.

You stayed a girl. Withered age was merely a mask. Your flirt was always on the fingertip as it pressed a hand, or placed a wedge of pie before a guest. You lived crossing the bridge into Canada. You never really learned you can't cross into lands where you aren't wanted. (Nor have I, really.) You never got the lice completely out of your hair. You couldn't cut cords of any kind. You never buried the placentas. Like a boy you played mumblety-peg and lost each time you played. What was your final happiness? Your father's grave. To know Ruth and Jennie were there watching the men shovel the earth. Your sisters admitted to loving you.

# GLOSSARY

Sweetgrass: Traditional Iroquois (Mohawk) basket woven from sweet-smelling grass of low northern country meadows.

Owl's Head: Formerly an office in which *Akwesasne Notes*, the Native American Journal, was edited by Jerry Gamble. Dorothy Thomas and Snowbird were volunteer workers.

Madame Jenika De Feriet: Early French emigre into northern New York State (c. 1816).

General Jacob Brown: Victorious hero in the battle at Sacketts Harbor, New York in the War of 1812.

"Drums," etc.: Pieces based on Mohawk "social dances" held in the winter in the Longhouse aiding in the perpetuation of the culture.

Turtle, Bear, Wolf: Three Mohawk clans at Akwasasne (St. Regis Reservation).

Strawberry: First natural fruit of the eastern spring. It is the symbol of life to Iroquois (Mohawk) people.

Wiliam Mothersell: Brother-in-law of the author.

Lance Henson: Contemporary Cheyenne poet living in Oklahoma.

Wejack: Abenaki word meaning groundhog or woodchuck.

Apache, Papago, Yuchi: Indian people from southwestern United States.

Little Voices: In traditional Iroquois story, these "little people" gave the wild strawberry and promised protection from bad spirits to the people because of a youth's generosity, his gift of food.

Peacemaker: A Huron who traveled to the Mohawks from the present day Canada. With the help of Aiionwatha he spread a new political philosophy and created the League of Nations, the Iroquois Confederacy of the Five Nations: Mohawk, Oneida, Cayuga, Onondaga, Seneca, and, later the Tuscarora. Little is known of him except that he had a bad stutter and might possibly have been driven from his own people, the Hurons, to their southern enemies, the Mohawks.

Atotarho: Onondaga chief who listened to the words, and *The Great Law of Peace*, of the Peacemaker through the persuasion of Aiionwatha. It remains to this day a hereditary Onondaga name of the leading chief who sits at the central Iroquois Council Fire at Onondaga.

Aiionwatha: Known in English as Hiawatha, not to be confused with the imposter of Longfellow's mythic edda, *Hiawatha*.

Ceremony of the Dark Waters: A healing ceremony.

Story Stone: From whence the Iroquois cultural stories allegedly came.

Snakes: The Mohawk Prophesy suggests two snakes, one silver and one gold, will devour the people village by village until at last a young boy arrives to slay them. They represent Canada and the United States.

Marquette: Jacques was a French Jesuit explorer who sought the head-waters of the Mississippi River.

Kiotsaeton: Mohawk chief who was sent to persuade the French Jesuits to return to Montreal. He was highly revered for his diplomacy and oratory. The Iroquois Confederacy wanted to avoid war with the French prompted mainly by the Seneca in the western part of what is now New York State, and demanded the Mohawk observe the *Great Law of Peace* and welcome the Jesuits as visitors in the land of the "White Pine," but, however, also to encourage the Blackrobes not to stay.

Jogues' Journal: There is a definite thought that Jogues was sent as a pawn by the French government to the Mohawk villages to scout not only numbers of warriors in the villages, but to keep a keen eye out for beaver pelts and other valued furs. Jogues may well have been duped in the veils of his religious ardor and zeal.

Bear: Mohawk moity, holding a strong religious persuasion. It was the Bear clan which demanded the Jesuits be put to death as a gesture of defiance to the French government. The Wolf and Turtle clans were not so adamantly disposed.

Jean de La Lande: Young lay novice who finally took the vows in respect for Jogues and in the fervor of devotion.

Sky-woman: From Iroquois Creation Story. She fell from the sky and was brought by the birds to rest on the back of a sea turtle. She was pregnant and soon gave birth to a girl-child whose sons, Right-handed Boy and Left-handed Boy, created the things of the world once their grandmother, through the help of muskrat, increased the size of the turtle's back and brought mud from the bottom of the sea to make earth.

Mary: The virgin mother of Jesus Christ.

Wolf Aunt: Her true name has been lost in the vagueries of history. She did not legally, in ceremony, adopt Isaac Jogues, but simply took him into her protective house and gave him bed and board. This was allowed as her own blood-son was dead.

Feast: It is not positively established whether Fathers Jogues and de La Lande were put to death in the village streets or at the lodge of Bear, a medicine person.

Visions: Isaac Jogues had two visions, one in the spring of 1642 and again in October 1642. The first told him he must die for his faith, and the second convinced him that the Mohawks were not mere cruel savages, but his ignorant brethern and in dire need of his missionary endeavors.

Rene Goupil: Jesuit who accompanied Jogues on the first journey into the Mohawk country. He was the first Jesuit to be put to death by the Mohawk. He was canonized as saint.

Tekakwitha (Kateri): Though it has been said her mother was Huron, Tekakwitha has been proclaimed the first Mohawk penitent. Her name was presented for canonization in 1932, better than 250 years after her death. She was beatified on June 22, 1980, in Rome by the Roman Catholic Church.

Aroniateka (Burning Sky): Mohawk chief and close friend to Colonel William Johnson. It was through this friendship that the Mohawks allied their Nation with the English.

Rokwaho: Means "Wolf-robe."

Born in 1929 between the St. Lawrence and Black Rivers, Maurice Kenny currently lives in Brooklyn where he co-edits the poetry journal *Contact/11* with J.G Gosciak; he is also the publisher of Strawberry Press. He has served as both panelist and advisor to many organizations, including P.E.N. For many years he has been associated with *Akwesasne Notes* and Studies in American Indian Literature. Guest speaker and poet at many national universities and art centers, he recently enjoyed a residency at The Writers Room in New York City. Apart from the collections in *Between Two Rivers*, Mr. Kenny is the author of *Is Summer This Bear* (1985), *Greyhounding This America* (1986), *Rain and Other Fictions* (1985), and a collection of historical essays, *Roman Nose and Other Essays* (1986). His work appears in many outstanding journals and anthologies, the latest being *The North Country* (Greenfield Review Press), *Harper's Book of 20th Century Native American Poetry (Harper & Row), Earth Power Coming* (Navajo Community College Press), *Wah' Kon Tah* (International Publishers), *Art Against Apartheid* (Ikon), and *I Tell You Now: Autobiographies of Native American Writers* (University of Nebraska). He edited *Wounds Beneath The Flesh (Blue Cloud Quaterly- 1983).*

*Blackrobe* was nominated for the Pulitzer in 1983 and was given the National Public Radio for Broadcasting Award. In 1984 he received the prestigious American Book Award for *The Mama Poems* (White Pine Press). Acclaimed by such critics as Robert Peters, Andrew Wiget, Geary Hobson, Michael Castro and Karl Kroeber, he was once quoted as having said, "I am committed to the earth and the past; to tradition and the future. I am committed to people and poetry." He is currently at work on a new collection of persona poems, *Tekonwatonti, Molly Brant: Poems of War.*

168